SAP® S/4HANA Fixed Asset Accounting Implementation Guide

Jerry Lucas

Thank you for purchasing this book from Espresso Tutorials!

Like a cup of espresso coffee, Espresso Tutorials SAP books are concise and effective. We know that your time is valuable and we deliver information in a succinct and straightforward manner. It only takes our readers a short amount of time to consume SAP concepts. Our books are well recognized in the industry for leveraging tutorial-style instruction and videos to show you step by step how to successfully work with SAP.

Check out our YouTube channel to watch our videos at *https://www.youtube.com/user/EspressoTutorials*.

If you are interested in SAP Finance and Controlling, join us at *http://www.fico-forum.com/forum2/* to get your SAP questions answered and contribute to discussions.

Related titles from Espresso Tutorials:

▶ Mary Loughran, Lennart Ullmann: **Guide to SAP® In-House Cash (ICH)**
   http://5191.espresso-tutorials.com

▶ Mary Loughran, Praveen Gupta: **Cash Management in SAP® S/4HANA**
   http://5281.espresso-tutorials.com

▶ Oona Flanagan: **A Practical Guide to SAP® S/4HANA Financial Accounting**
   http://5320.espresso-tutorials.com

▶ Oona Flanagan: **Delta from SAP ERP Financials to SAP® S/4HANA Finance**
   http://5321.espresso-tutorials.com

▶ Kees van Westerop: **New Fixed Asset Accounting in SAP® S/4HANA**
   http://5409.espresso-tutorials.com

▶ Maddie Allenspach: **First Steps in Financial Accounting in SAP® S/4HANA**
   http://5410.espresso-tutorials.com

▶ Mary Loughran, Praveen Gupta: **Bank Communication Management in SAP® S/4HANA**
   http://5469.espresso-tutorials.com

**The SAP eBook Library:
Team and Company Access**

Did you know that you can provide your team with effective
SAP training with access to the SAP eBook Library and
reduce travel and training costs? You can!

Curious about how we stack up against the competition?

	Espresso Tutorials	Other Offerings
Price per Year	**$159 annually**	**$699 annually**
SAP eBooks	✓	✓
SAP video tutorials	✓	✗
Mobile app	✓	✓
Immediate access to new titles	✓	✓
Self service to maintain users (for companies)	✓	✗

Pricing available for teams of 5+. A team of 10 can access the library for one year for
$850 (pre-tax). That's a 42% discount. The larger your team, the more you save.

Try a free 7-day, no obligation trial:
http://free.espresso-tutorials.com

Get a quote for your team today:
http://company.espresso-tutorials.com

Jerry Lucas
SAP® S/4HANA Fixed Asset Accounting Implementation Guide

ISBN:	978-3-960-12101-5
Editor:	Lisa Jackson
Cover Design:	Philip Esch
Cover Photo:	istockphoto.com | No. 175998020
Interior Book Design:	Tanja Jahns

All rights reserved.

1st Edition 2021, Gleichen

© 2021 by Espresso Tutorials GmbH

URL: *www.espresso-tutorials.com*

Feedback
We greatly appreciate any feedback you may have concerning this book. Please send your feedback via email to: *info@espresso-tutorials.com*.

Table of Contents

Preface

The purpose of this book is to help you navigate through the Asset Accounting Implementation Guide in SAP S/4HANA. There are lots of screenshots to help illustrate or view standard SAP functionality as well as depictions showing some customizing options in Asset Accounting.

By reading through this book, and reviewing the screenshots, I hope you can gain a deeper understanding of how to configure Asset Accounting in SAP S/4HANA. And, as you gain a better understanding, then you will also hopefully get more comfortable with your overall knowledge and awareness of how all of the pieces of the puzzle fit together. When I think back to my very first SAP project, and my first opportunity to configure Asset Accounting in SAP, it was daunting. I leaned heavily on my team members and associates who were more senior than I, and I tried to get as much help as I could, without overstretching that need for assistance.

At some point, the struggle to figure out how to configure certain functionality leads to a level of understanding that you don't achieve if someone tells you the answer. So, I tried to keep a healthy balance of trying to figure things out for myself, and then when I could not, I decided to reach out for help. I hope you can use this book as a helpful resource in your journey to understanding SAP Asset Accounting. In some ways, I am hoping this book can pay forward the help I received.

Overall, I hope you will find some useful insights and gain a better understanding of SAP Asset Accounting as seen through the lens of the *SAP Implementation Guide*. I hope that my experience will help you to have a smooth go live, or an uneventful implementation, or maybe even a combination of both.

We have added a few icons to highlight important information. These include:

Tips

Tips highlight information that provides more details about the subject being described and/or additional background information.

Attention

Attention notices highlight information that you should be aware of when you go through the examples in this book on your own.

Finally, a note concerning the copyright: all screenshots printed in this book are the copyright of SAP SE. All rights are reserved by SAP SE. Copyright pertains to all SAP images in this publication. For the sake of simplicity, we do not mention this specifically underneath every screenshot.

1 Intro to SAP Asset Accounting configuration

Companies use SAP Asset Accounting to manage fixed and intangible assets for compulsory statutory reporting. Statutory reporting can be defined as both local reporting and group reporting. Statutory reporting is required for the legal entity (usually the company code of the assets) that owns the asset.

In a scenario where you have a single legal entity that has the same local and reporting currencies, and no unique consolidation requirements, reporting for local and group can be the same currency, such as local currency. In another scenario, local reporting can be in one currency, such as LOCAL CURRENCY and group reporting can be in a currency of the consolidated company, or the Group Company with a separate reporting currency, in GROUP CURRENCY. Figure 1.1 shows the sample company code has USD as the LOCAL CURRENCY, and has EUR as the GROUP CURRENCY. This setting is found in the Financial Accounting Global Settings. It is not part of the SAP Asset Accounting IMG, but it has a profound impact on the currencies used in SAP Asset Accounting.

Figure 1.1: Company code settings for the ledger

The *chart of depreciation* is the most important, and the highest level, of the SAP Asset Accounting hierarchy. The chart of depreciation is defined based on country-specific requirements. If you have two companies in a corporate group, and they are in two separate countries, then you will need to have two separate charts of depreciation. The chart of depreciation is assigned to the company code in the configuration, and the chart of depreciation contains all the currencies, depreciation areas, depreciation methods, and requirements for that specific country. In the case of multiple company codes in the same country, the company codes will share the same chart of depreciation, and all the associated characteristics of that chart of depreciation.

This book will ultimately help you decide how to configure the charts of depreciation, the company codes, and the currencies necessary for the different depreciation areas, and the potentially numerous depreciation keys needed to record monthly depreciation or amortization for your specific company. This book also covers the potential needs for multiple or single ledgers based on different reporting needs of the company code.

1.1 What is SAP Asset Accounting?

SAP *Asset Accounting* is the management of fixed assets and intangible assets that belong to a single company code. Assets can be further divided into asset classes, which provide specific default values for asset master records and reporting requirements. For example, fixed assets like autos, software, hardware, and buildings can all be different asset classes, with different defaults for useful life and depreciation keys. Additionally, intangible assets are similar in that way, with different classes for goodwill, intellectual property, trademarks, and copyrights, to name a few. At the end of the reporting period, the assets will have depreciation calculated and posted to the General Ledger, and also the Asset Accounting subledger. Similar to Accounts Payable and Accounts Receivable, Asset Accounting will have its own subledger for which to track the value of the different assets and classes.

In addition to keeping track of the asset master records, SAP uses account determination to keep track to the required General Ledger accounts that are linked to the assets for use in financial reporting. SAP uses the account determination to use the same account for cost, accumulated depreciation, depreciation expense, gain or loss on asset disposal, and clearing accounts associated with asset classes. These General Ledger (G/L) accounts will contain the daily and periodic postings which will make up the fixed assets valuations for the balance sheet. Additionally, the G/L accounts will be posted to for potentially different accounting methods like US GAAP or IFRS, and these different methods will be updated in different account ledgers. These ledgers are commonly referred to as the leading ledger and the local ledger, but these are only two potential ledgers; there can also be more than two ledgers.

1.2 Functions of SAP Asset Accounting

There are many functions available in SAP Asset Accounting, and you can divide them into three main groups: Master Data, Transactional data, and

Valuation reporting. Master data refers to the company codes, cost centers, WBS elements, depreciation keys, etc. Transaction Data refers to monthly depreciation entries, acquisition entries, subsequent acquisition entries, transfer entries, and disposal or retirement entries. Valuation reporting will encompass the need for reporting asset balances.

SAP Asset Accounting reports can be divided into separate types of reporting characteristics:

- ▶ Master data
- ▶ Transactional data
- ▶ Valuation reporting

Companies look to asset reporting to answer questions like: "How many assets do I have?", "Where are my assets located?", and "How much are my assets worth?" within Local Currency or in Group Currency. Also, asset reports will answer questions like, how much did I 'spend' this quarter on asset acquisitions, how 'many' disposals took place, what was the 'value' of disposals, and even 'what was the sales revenue generated by those disposals, if any'. Each of these types of questions can be asked and answered with standard asset reports. SAP has many standard asset reports that cover each of the characteristic groups mentioned earlier. Additionally, SAP provides the ability to customize the standard asset reporting output via asset history sheet versions.

SAP is able to report on the different types of transactions posted to assets by assigning a specific transaction type to each asset transaction. Additionally, the transaction type can also contain a consolidation transaction type, for use in consolidations (outside the scope of this book). When these transaction types are posted into the asset master and subsequently the different depreciation areas and ledgers, in some cases, the transaction type will only post to a single ledger or area. This is very helpful in the case of an international company that consolidates in a reporting currency different from the local reporting currency. The consolidated group may need to keep the asset valuation on the company's consolidated books, but not on the local ledger's books, and setting up special transaction types to do this is a great function in SAP Asset Accounting.

Assets under construction are another popular function of SAP Asset Accounting. These special types of fixed assets get their own designated asset classes, and their own special accounting methods and handling. Assets under construction can be linked to other objects in SAP like internal orders, or Work Breakdown Structures, also known as WBS elements. Linking of assets under construction to other objects like internal orders, opens up the ability to handle special projects, specialized reporting, and the flexibility to delay the capitalization of assets to when they are completely 'built'—either internally or externally—with multiple vendors or entities, and eventually placed in service.

Leased assets are also a big concern, with the new rules and regulations surrounding off-book leasing and getting the assets onto the financial statements so they can be tracked and valuated according to the new rules. Leased assets can be maintained in both SAP and external systems, with the external systems driving the leasing calculations and interfacing with SAP for valuation tracking. Reporting can be done from both systems, but monthly depreciation and amortization can still be achieved via the standard SAP depreciation run.

Another type of special asset class is low-value assets, or LVAs, which can keep track of asset records that are not wanted on the books, or are expensed immediately in the period acquired, but are important for record keeping by the company.

1.2.1 Depreciation run and periodic posting

One of the most important functions of SAP Asset Accounting is the ability to run monthly depreciation for the assets in the SAP system. The ability to post depreciation for hundreds, thousands, or millions of assets at month end is a thing of beauty. In addition to posting depreciation for the assets in a local currency for book depreciation, depending on how many depreciation areas there are in the chart of depreciation, there can be many depreciation area postings at month end for multiple statutory reasons, and in multiple ledgers.

Most of the SAP Asset Accounting support issues will revolve around the depreciation run at month end. One of the goals of this book is to provide a configuration strategy to help people make important, key decisions on how to set up the chart of depreciation, company codes, and depreciation areas to minimize support issues once the company is live on SAP Asset Accounting.

The depreciation run will run smoothly provided the settings are correct and the configuration is robust enough to support the many variables that companies see during the month and year. In order for depreciation to run smoothly, many objects need to be synchronized and in harmony. These items are covered in great detail throughout this book.

One of the advantages of moving to SAP S/4HANA for Asset Accounting is the ability to post in several ledgers in real time, and avoid the extra steps involved at month end for periodic postings. In older versions of SAP, it was necessary to run the periodic posting program to synchronize the General Ledger with the SAP Asset Ledger. This extra step to synchronize the ledgers becomes irrelevant with the new Asset Accounting in SAP S/4HANA. This benefit cannot be overstated due to various reasons for month-end processing, multiple transaction postings, and multiple ledgers. This new functionality will bring peace of mind to your asset accounting, without the need to worry about periodic postings and having to do the extra processing step at month end.

One of the most dramatic improvements to Asset Accounting in SAP S/4HANA is the introduction of the ACDOCA table. The *ACDOCA* table is a new line item table for financial postings, and it contains many types of ledger postings that were in different tables in ECC. You can think of it as a new and improved BSEG table that combines assets, segments, profit centers, cost centers, etc. It is a combination of FI and CO postings. Also, if you are the type of analyst that prefers to look up table entries, you can still use SE16 or SE16N to view postings in ACDOCA. You will see segment postings, profit center entries, cost center entries, asset ledger postings, and many other financial postings.

The new ACDOCA table enables a stronger link between asset accounting and the General Ledger. It also allows for real time posting of assets in the Asset Accounting Ledger and General Ledger. Because of this, we do not need to run the periodic posting program at month end to bring ledgers into balance and reconciliation. To reiterate, in ECC in the past, if you had two depreciation areas that posted to different ledgers, you would need to run the periodic posting program during month end. Now, with real-time postings in ACDOCA, you can find both ledger entries in ACDOCA, but you will not need to run the AFBP transaction to bring the ledgers into balance at month end, since the postings will be made in real time. Another benefit you will find is when you review the asset explorer balances, they will be the same as the G/L balances. You will not need to wait to see the month-end entries posted by the AFBP transaction. You will still need to run the depreciation program, and this will be covered later in Chapter 5.

For more info on the ACDOCA table and how it works with other areas and modules outside of asset accounting, visit the SAP online help. It is beyond the scope of this book to cover all the technical aspects and improvements.

1.3 Multiple depreciation areas and valuations

A chart of depreciation is separated into different sections or valuations which SAP has named depreciation areas. Each depreciation area has its own currency, currency type, depreciation key, useful life, etc. There are many more characteristics to be found in each depreciation area, and they can be duplicated over several depreciation areas for a single asset.

Generally speaking, asset depreciation areas are tied to valuation for the asset. The book and local depreciation areas are both Area 01. Depreciation areas are only recorded in a single currency, so if more than one currency is needed for reporting, then you will need more than one depreciation area.

In previous versions of SAP and Asset Accounting, the depreciation run was limited in how many depreciation areas it could post. This necessitated an additional program that would have to run after depreciation posted, to synchronize the additional depreciation areas and the ledgers linked to those depreciation areas. With the SAP S/4HANA version, the depreciation run is now set up to post to multiple depreciation areas and multiple ledgers at the same time, or in the same run in real time. Previously, SAP required the periodic processing program to be run, also known as transaction codes ASKB or ASKBN, to post to the multiple ledgers and depreciation areas.

1.4 SAP Asset Accounting reporting

One of the most important aspects or requirements for SAP Asset Accounting is the reporting of the assets and their associated values. Each depreciation area will record values for the asset in the currency type and currency code defined for that depreciation area.

Master data reports will provide lists for assets that are found in different cost centers, WBS elements, functional areas, locations, and more. Transaction data reports will provide reporting on acquisitions, additional acquisitions, planned depreciation, unplanned depreciation, transfers, and eventual end of life for assets with retirements or disposals.

With an asset history sheet, companies can create customized reports to handle the various needs that arise for companies and countries. The asset history sheet is part of the configuration, and will be covered later on in this book, in Chapter 9 Information systems.

2 Organizational structures

This chapter covers all the organizational structures needed to con-figure SAP Asset Accounting. It reviews charts of depreciation, compa-ny codes, number ranges, account determination, screen layouts and rules, chart-of-depreciation-dependent configurations, and the assign-ment of many of these items.

2.1 Organizational structures in Asset Accounting

The following sections review the different objects in Asset Accounting and how they combine together in SAP Asset Accounting. Upon finishing this chapter, you should be more adept at understanding how a chart of de-preciation is used within a company code. You should also understand how account determination reveals the General Ledger accounts used in the automatic account determination when posting to assets. You should also better understand how the screen layout determines the fields you see in your Asset Accounting master records.

2.1.1 Check country-specific settings

The check country-specific settings section shows which country charts of depreciation are available. You can copy the settings to a new chart and start assigning company codes. Also, if you drill down to the detail of a country code, you can update the values for the *low-value asset*, which is the amount for classified assets that are low enough in value to depreciate immediately, usually in the first period the asset is placed in service. This is usually done for assets that are not relevant in value, but have other in-trinsic values, so much so that the asset is worth tracking in SAP Asset Ac-counting. This section also covers how the depreciation key switches to a new phase and what this means for depreciation of the asset. There are dif-ferent changeover methods which determine how depreciation is affected in each phase. Figure 2.1 displays the country information for COUNTRY KEY US.

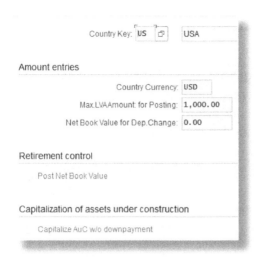

Figure 2.1: Asset accounting country information

2.1.2 Copy reference chart of depreciation and depreciation areas

Sometimes you need a customized chart of depreciation to suit business needs. If you find yourself in this position, copy one of the SAP standard charts and create a new one, so that it can be customized and assigned to the company codes in need of the special chart of depreciation. Figure 2.2 shows how to copy one chart of depreciation to another chart of depreciation.

Figure 2.2: Copy chart of depreciation to company code

2.1.3 Assign chart of depreciation to company code

Assigning the chart of depreciation to the company code(s) is essential to starting SAP Asset Accounting functionality for the company code(s). This step in a configuration is what effectively activates Asset Accounting for the company code. Without the chart of depreciation assignment, there will be no Asset Accounting in that company code. Figure 2.3 shows how charts of depreciation are assigned to each company code.

‹ SAP		Change View "Maintain company code in Asset Accounting": Overview

| ∨ ↺ | ≝ ≝ ≝ ⦿ | More ∨ |

CoCd	Company Name	Chrt dep	Description
1010	Hamburg	1010	Chart of Depreciation 1010 DE
1011	Fair Trade Coffee GmbH	ZDE1	Chart of Depreciation ZDE1 DE
1020	Green Bike GmbH	1010	Chart of Depreciation 1010 DE
1110	Fish and Chips Company	1110	Chart of Depreciation 1110 GB
1210	Société Data	1210	Chart of Depreciation 1210 FR
1310	Shanghai Shoes Co	1310	Chart of Depreciation 1310 CN
1510	Tokyo Tots Co	1510	Chart of Depreciation 1510 JP
1710	California Data Ltd	1710	Chart of Depreciation 1710 US
3010	Down Under Data, Inc	3010	Chart of Depreciation 3010 AU

Figure 2.3: Assign chart to company codes

2.1.4 Specify number assignment across company codes

When choosing to have number assignments for the Asset Master Records, you can customize how those numbers are generated across the company codes in the system. By choosing the same company code as the one for assignment of number ranges, the asset numbers will be unique to the company code. If one company code is chosen as the source for many company code number ranges, then the asset numbers will be unique across the system and those same company codes. This is because several company codes will be drawing from the same number ranges. Figure 2.4 shows each company code assigned its own number range, so asset numbers will be unique to each company code, but not unique across the system. Alternatively, if you assigned the same company code here for the number ranges, then you would be using one number range and there would be no duplication of asset numbers across these company codes. Keep in mind, the combination of the company code and asset number will make the asset record unique in the SAP system.

Figure 2.4: Specify number assignment across company codes

2.2 Asset classes

Asset classes are the main building blocks for assets and are how you define the different types of assets found in the company code and system. With an asset class, you can define many characteristics for the assets created in that class. Additionally, you can define default values for the characteristics based on the type of asset you are creating and recording. For example, you can default in location codes for assets in specific asset classes. Let's say for example, one company buys Machinery and Equipment, and all these assets will end up in the same location. You can default in the location code, tax jurisdiction codes (if US-based or a company code that uses tax jurisdiction codes), evaluation group data, etc.

2.2.1 Specify account determination

Account determination is the definition of General Ledger accounts across both the asset class and chart of depreciation. Figure 2.5 shows the account determination and the description associated with each one.

Acct. determ.	Name of Account Determination
160010	Buildings
160020	Machinery and Equipment
160030	Leasehold Imrovements
160040	Vehicles
160050	Office Equipment
160060	Furniture and Fixtures
160070	Computer Hardware
160080	Computer Software
160090	Assets under Construction
160200	Low Value Assets
193300	Goodwill

Figure 2.5: Specify account determination

2.2.2 Create screen layout rules

Screen layout rules are used to determine which fields are shown in which asset class. You can define a different screen layout for each asset class or use the same screen layout rule for all asset classes. Once the screen layout is defined, you can then assign it to the asset class.

Following the earlier example, this is where you can create a special screen layout. Figure 2.6 shows Y311 Vehicles US, and it is a copy of Y310 for VEHICLES. The example is for a US-based country layout for vehicles, but the screen layout can be specific or unique for other reasons or business needs. Figure 2.6 contains the list of screen layouts and the associated names of the layout rule.

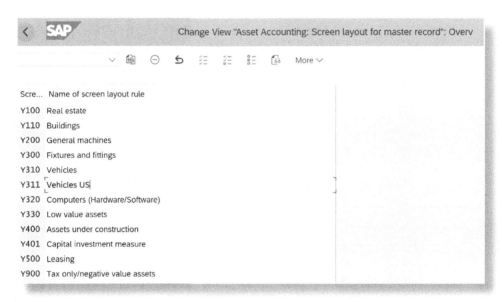

Figure 2.6: Screen layout for master record

2.2.3 Define number range interval

In this section, you create number ranges for each asset class. You can assign all assets to the same number range, or you can create separate number ranges for each asset class. You need to consider the volume of assets in the asset class when creating the asset number ranges, so that you do not run out of numbers in the volume range of asset master records in that asset class. Another thing to consider is the typing involved

21

for the asset numbers when Accounts Payable may need to enter them in the invoice, or when accounting personnel are looking up asset master records for various research needs. The smaller the actual number in digits would be a great benefit or hindrance to data entry, on many levels, so it is something to consider. Figure 2.7 shows the number range, and the actual 'from' and 'to' ranges associated. The number range status is also shown. Note that when zero is shown, no master records have been created yet. The check box on the far right delineates an external number range.

‹ SAP		Edit Intervals: Asset Number, Object ANLAGENNR, Subobject 1510		
∨ 6⟩ ⁙ More ∨				
No From No.	To Number	NR Status	Ext	
01 000000100000	000000199999	0	☐	
02 000000200000	000000299999	0	☐	
03 000000300000	000000399999	0	☐	
04 000000400000	000000499999	0	☐	
05 000000500000	000000599999	0	☐	
06 000000600000	000000699999	600000	☐	
07 000000700000	000000799999	0	☐	
08 000000800000	000000899999	0	☐	
09 000000900000	000000999999	0	☐	
90 A	D	0	☑	
99 000000000001	000000099999	0	☑	

Figure 2.7: Define number ranges

2.2.4   Define asset classes

There are standard asset classes in SAP, but many companies like to adjust the names to better suit the needs of their business. Figure 2.8 shows the asset class SHORT TEXT name, ASSET CLASS DESCRIPTION, NAME OF ACCOUNT DETERMINATION, and NAME OF SCREEN LAYOUT RULE for the class.

Class	Short Text	Asset Class Description	Name of Account Determination	Name of screen layout rule
1000	Real Estate (Land)	Real Estate (Land)	Land and Land Improvements	Real estate
1100	Buildings	Buildings	Buildings	Buildings
1200	Land Improvements	Land Improvements	Land and Land Improvements	Real estate
1500	Leasehold Improvmnts	Leasehold Improvements	Leasehold Imrovements	Buildings
2000	Machinery Equipment	Machinery and Equipment	Machinery and Equipment	General machines
3000	Fixtures Fittings	Fixtures and Fittings	Furniture and Fixtures	Fixtures and fittings
3100	Vehicles Owned	Vehicles Owned	Vehicles	Vehicles
3110	Vehicles Leased	Vehicles Leased	Vehicles	Vehicles

Figure 2.8: Define asset classes

2.2.5 Specify chart-of-depreciation-dependent screen layout and account assignment

Using the combination of chart of depreciation and the screen layout, you can customize a unique layout for the company code(s) utilizing the chart of depreciation and the asset classes assigned to the screen layout. You can also adjust the account determination when you need to make modifications based on special requirements from the business.

Figure 2.9 shows chart-of-depreciation-independent data assigned to a screen layout of Y310 and account determination of 160040. But, for this combination of ASSET CLASS 3100 and chart of depreciation 1510, you can set up control entries for the SCREEN LAYOUT RULE of Y311 and ACCOUNT DETERMINATION of 160045. So, with this configuration option, you can slightly adjust the ASSET CLASS in this chart of depreciation, where all company codes assigned to 1510 will follow this configuration setup.

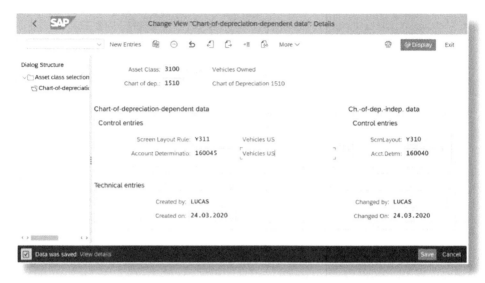

Figure 2.9: Chart-of-depreciation-dependent data

2.3 Country-specific functions

Country-specific functions are unique to the country involved, and usually are statutory requirements defined for specialized reporting needs. If your country is not listed here, you can generally ignore the section.

2.3.1 Maintain asset types

It is always a good idea to contact a local SAP consultant to get help with local or statutory configuration settings. They are usually the most knowledgeable and are worth the extra expense with the consulting advice provided in the long term. For instance, in the MAINTAIN ASSET TYPES section, the asset type is used for selecting Russian asset reports and is therefore considered a local setting, or country-specific setting. Figure 2.10 shows the ASSET CLASS, with ASSET TYPE, VALUATION TYPE, valuation class (VALCL), equipment category, functional location category, and WAREHOUSE checkbox.

Figure 2.10: Maintain asset types

3 Integration with the General Ledger

This chapter covers SAP Asset Accounting and the ledger's integration with the General Ledger, or with multiple ledgers. For example, a company may have a leading ledger (0L) and a local ledger (1L). The 0L is usually tied to Depreciation Area 01, and the 1L is tied to Depreciation Area 02, or another area.

3.1 Integration with the General Ledger

Most of this chapter, and the configuration it covers, depends directly on how the chart of depreciation is set up, and how and what is posted into the General Ledger, or to the leading ledger and local leading ledgers. Another term that can be used to refer to the local ledger is the non-leading ledger. These terms can sometimes be used interchangeably to reference the same ledger.

One minor note: once you log in to SAP and enter the IMG, if you have not selected a chart of depreciation, SAP will use a pop-up window to set the current chart of depreciation for your session. Figure 3.1 shows that chart of depreciation 1710 is chosen for the configuration changes.

Figure 3.1: Determine work area—entry

If you ever need to change the current chart of depreciation to another chart of depreciation while in the IMG for configuration purposes, please see Figure 4.1: Chart of depreciation selection.

3.1.1 Define how depreciation areas post to the General Ledger

Figure 3.2 shows how the different depreciation areas will post (or not post) to the G/L. For example, Depreciation Area 01 will always post to the General Ledger, and this will happen in the company code currency, which is defined in the configuration of currencies in the General Ledger. In contrast, the group depreciation area will usually be set up to take the same values, converted, and then posted in group currency. You will also have the option to set up depreciation areas that only periodically post to the G/L, or are only 'statistical' depreciation areas that only track the asset values for reporting purposes, and do not post to any ledger. One example of a statistical depreciation area that usually would never post to a ledger would be a tax depreciation area. Usually, tax depreciation areas in the US are only used for tracking asset values for tax depreciation purposes, and do not have additional ledgers outside of SAP Asset Accounting.

Define Depreciation Areas

Ar.	Name of Depreciation Area	Real	Trgt Group	Acc.Princ.	G/L	
1	Book Depreciation	✓	2L	LG	Area Posts in Real Time	⌄
2	Book Depreciation	✓	2L	LG	Area Does Not Post	⌄
30	Local GAAP-local currency	✓	2L	LG	Area Does Not Post	⌄
32	IFRS in local currency	✓	0L	IFRS	Area Posts in Real Time	⌄
33	IFRS in group currency	✓	0L	IFRS	Area Does Not Post	⌄
34	Local GAAP-Group currency	✓	2L	LG	Area Does Not Post	⌄
90	Federal Tax ACRS/MACRS	✓	2L	LG	Area Does Not Post	⌄
91	Alternative Minimum Tax	✓	2L	LG	Area Does Not Post	⌄
92	Adjusted Current Earnings	✓	2L	LG	Area Does Not Post	⌄
93	Corporate Earnings & Profits	✓	2L	LG	Area Does Not Post	⌄
94	Special Valuations	✓	2L	LG	Area Does Not Post	⌄

Figure 3.2: Define depreciation areas

In addition to defining how the depreciation areas post to other ledgers, you can also define what is posting in the depreciation areas in SAP Asset Accounting. Figure 3.3 shows each value that is allowed for posting. For example, the ACQUISITION VALUE will allow positive values or zero, but will not allow negative values. So, once our asset has a debit balance, some credits can be posted to the asset, but the total acquisition value must be positive or zero.

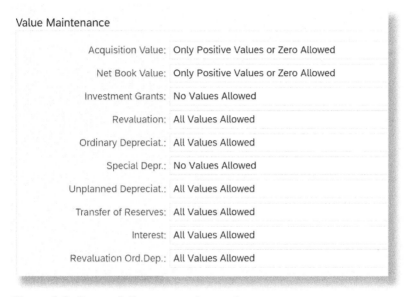

Value Maintenance

Acquisition Value:	Only Positive Values or Zero Allowed
Net Book Value:	Only Positive Values or Zero Allowed
Investment Grants:	No Values Allowed
Revaluation:	All Values Allowed
Ordinary Depreciat.:	All Values Allowed
Special Depr.:	No Values Allowed
Unplanned Depreciat.:	All Values Allowed
Transfer of Reserves:	All Values Allowed
Interest:	All Values Allowed
Revaluation Ord.Dep.:	All Values Allowed

Figure 3.3: Depreciation area value maintenance

3.1.2 Assign G/L accounts

The Assign G/L Accounts section is where you enter the G/L balance sheet and expense accounts that are used for acquisitions, depreciation, retirements, and transfers, among several other types of postings. Figure 3.4 shows the chart of accounts and account determination depreciation areas that are ready for G/L account assignments.

Figure 3.5 shows the account assignment for ACQUISITION, and which accounts are used. You can also see the RETIREMENT accounts for this account determination and depreciation area.

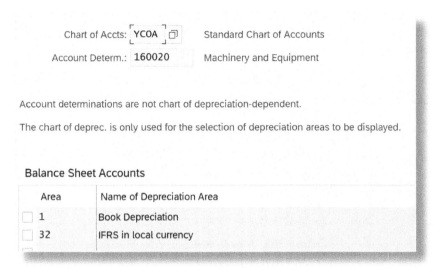

Figure 3.4: Assign G/L accounts

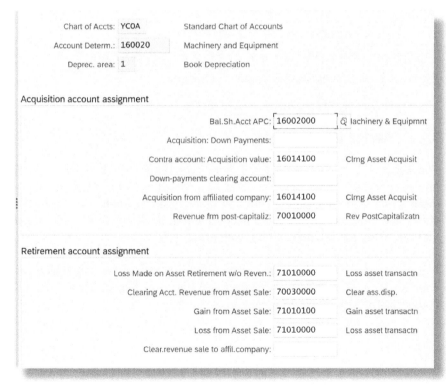

Figure 3.5: Assign G/L accounts for acquisition

Additionally, if you have an asset depreciation area that is set up for REVA-LUATION, you can enter the account here. Figure 3.6 shows a place holder for the G/L account used in posting revaluation entries.

Revaluation account assignment

Revaluation Acquis. and Production Costs:	16002000	Machinery & Equipmnt
Offsetting Account: Revaluation APC:		

Account assignment of cost portions not capitalized

Cost elem. for settlmt AuC to CO objects:		
Capital. difference/Non-operatng expense:		

Balance sheet accounts

Clearing of Investment Support:	26911000	Clrg invst rcvbl rcd

Refund accounts

Repayment of Investment Support:		
Expense: Repayment of Invest.Support:		

Figure 3.6: Assign G/L accounts for revaluation

The depreciation section shows the expense accounts where the depreciation or amortization will be posted for each account determination and depreciation area combination. See Figure 3.7.

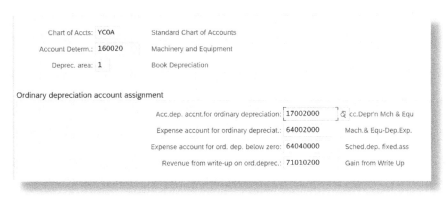

Figure 3.7: Assign G/L accounts for depreciation

In addition to the ordinary depreciation posted to an asset, you can also identify the unplanned depreciation accounts, reserve accounts, revaluation accounts, and interest accounts. This is shown in Figure 3.8.

Unplanned depreciation account assignment

Accumulated dep. account unpl. deprec.:	17002000	Acc.Depr'n Mch & Equ
Expense account for unplanned deprec.:	64030000	Unsched.dep.Expense
P&LAct.Unpl.Dep.Below 0:	64030000	Unsched.dep.Expense
Revenue from write-up on unplnd. deprec.:	71010200	Gain from Write Up

Account assignment for transfer of reserves

Val. adj. acct. for transfer of reserves:		
Contra account for transferring reserves:		
Revenue from w-up transfer of reserves:		

Account assignment for revaluation on depreciation

Reval. accumulated ord. depreciation:	17002000	Acc.Depr'n Mch & Equ
Offsetting accnt: Reval. ordinary deprc.:	71015000	OffsetAcct Reval Dep

Interest account assignment

Expense account for interest:		
Clearing interest posting:		
Intrst expense when book val.below zero:		

Figure 3.8: Assign G/L accounts for unplanned depreciation

3.2 Technical clearing account for integrated acquisitions

When using clearing accounts for integrated acquisitions, you can identify the account in the configuration. There are two very important notes regarding the technical clearing account. One, this account must be a balance sheet item, and it must also be a reconciliation account, which means it cannot be posted manually. Two, the account must not be used in the Asset Accounting account determination.

I have seen many times over the years where this account is not set up as a reconciliation account, and it causes all kinds of problems for G/L and Asset

Accounting teams at period end. Be sure to put this account on your check list when setting up new company codes or activating Asset Accounting for the first time in a company code. Figure 3.9 shows where this account gets assigned.

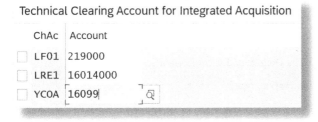

Technical Clearing Account for Integrated Acquisition

ChAc	Account
LF01	219000
LRE1	16014000
YCOA	16099

Figure 3.9: Assign G/L accounts for integrated acquisition

3.3 Integrated transactions

In the next configuration nodes, you have the option to post derived document types for ledger-specific postings.

3.3.1 Specify alternative document type for accounting-principle-specific documents

Figure 3.10 shows the original document type is AA. When you want to refer to accounting principle documents, you will use a derived document type of AP (not to be confused with the AP acronym for Accounts Payable). The document type choice is up to you, so pick one that makes sense.

General/Company-Code-Independent Doc. Type Determination

Original Doc. Type	Derived Doc. Type	
AA	AP	

Figure 3.10: Assign derived document type

31

3.3.2   Define separate document types by company code

In the case where you need or desire a different document type for specific ledgers, then you need to specify different company codes. If no derived document type is entered, then the system will use the original document type. Figure 3.11 shows where the derived document type is assigned to the company code.

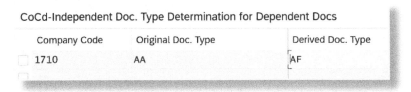

CoCd-Independent Doc. Type Determination for Dependent Docs

Company Code	Original Doc. Type	Derived Doc. Type
☐ 1710	AA	AF

Figure 3.11: Assign derived document type by company code

3.4   Specify posting key

You will also confirm the posting keys used for the default posting of asset values. The most common of the asset posting keys will be 70 for debit and 75 for credit. There can be others, but these are the two most common, and this is like the posting keys 40 and 50 for debit and credit in the General Ledger. Figure 3.12 shows where to assign the posting keys.

Transaction: ANL   Asset posting

Posting Key

Debit: 70 ⌕

Credit: 75

Note: Posting keys are independent of chart of accounts

Figure 3.12: Specify posting keys

3.5 Field status variants

Changing the *field status variants* (FSV) may be necessary for various reasons. Be careful not to confuse these with another FSV, financial statement versions; they are very different in terms of functionality. You should have a specific field status variant for your asset reconciliation in the General Ledger, where specific asset characteristics are available, optional, or required. The FSV that is ultimately used by the asset G/L accounts should be considered and reviewed by your G/L team members to ensure the appropriateness. Some things to consider in the FSV for asset accounting are having the asset retirement and asset number as optional and not hidden, for the sort variant. Figure 3.13 shows the setup for a generic FSV for an asset reconciliation balance sheet account, in the ASSET ACCOUNTING section of field status variants.

Figure 3.13: Field status variants

3.6 Assign tax indicator

Assign tax indicators enable the input of default tax codes for non-taxable and taxable transactions. Please see Figure 3.14 showing tax codes assigned to company codes, and in some cases the jurisdiction code, too.

CoCd	Company Name	City	Input Ta...	Output T...	Jurisdict. Co...
1710	California Data Ltd	Palo Alto	I0	O0	7700000000
3010	Down Under Data, Inc	Melbourne	P0	S0	

Figure 3.14: Assign tax indicator

3.7 Specify financial statement versions

Financial statement versions are used in the G/L to organize and present financial statements. This is where a balance sheet or cash flow statement can be built, and the financial statement version is assigned to asset accounting. When using asset accounting reports, this FSV is used for presenting the assets and their balances. Figure 3.15 shows where to find the financial statement version assignment for each depreciation area.

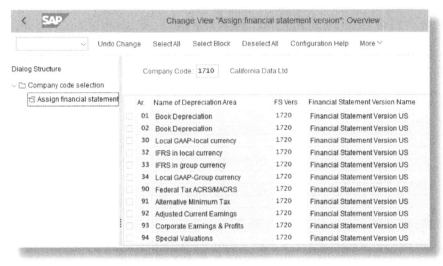

Figure 3.15: Assign financial statement version

3.8 Post depreciation to General Ledger accounting

Assigning the document for posting depreciation, usually the AF (depreciation posting) document type is used here. Review Figure 3.16 to see which document type is assigned for depreciation postings.

		Undo Change	Select All	Select Block	Deselect All	Confi

CoCode	Company Name	Doc.Type	Description
1010	Hamburg	AF	Depreciation Pstngs
1011	Fair Trade Coffee GmbH	AF	Depreciation Pstngs
1012	Fair Trade Coffee GmbH	AF	Depreciation Pstngs
1013	Fair Trade Coffee SARL	AF	Depreciation Pstngs
1020	Green Bike GmbH	AF	Depreciation Pstngs
1110	Fish and Chips Company	AF	Depreciation Pstngs
1210	Société Data	AF	Depreciation Pstngs

Figure 3.16: Assign document type for depreciation posting

3.8.1 Specify document type for posting of depreciation

You can define document types and also assign the document type for depreciation postings. Figure 3.16 illustrates what you need to accomplish for each company code and document type assignment.

3.8.2 Doc type for cross-company-code cost accounting

Setting up the document type AF (depreciation type) for cross-company-code accounting is only necessary if this functionality is configured. It is advisable to use the AF document type here, as with the previous configuration, and this is shown in Figure 3.17.

Document Type for Cross-Company-Code Cost Accounting

TType	Transaction Type Name	Document Type	Description
500	Post depreciation	AF	Depreciation Pstngs

Figure 3.17: Assign document type for cross-company code

35

3.8.3 Specify intervals and posting rules

The next step is to determine when to post depreciation. Most commonly, depreciation is posted monthly, but other periods can be defined and used for periodic postings. You also set the posting area for interest, revaluation, or below zero when the useful life ends (not common). Figure 3.18 shows the MONTHLY POSTING chosen for the period and method.

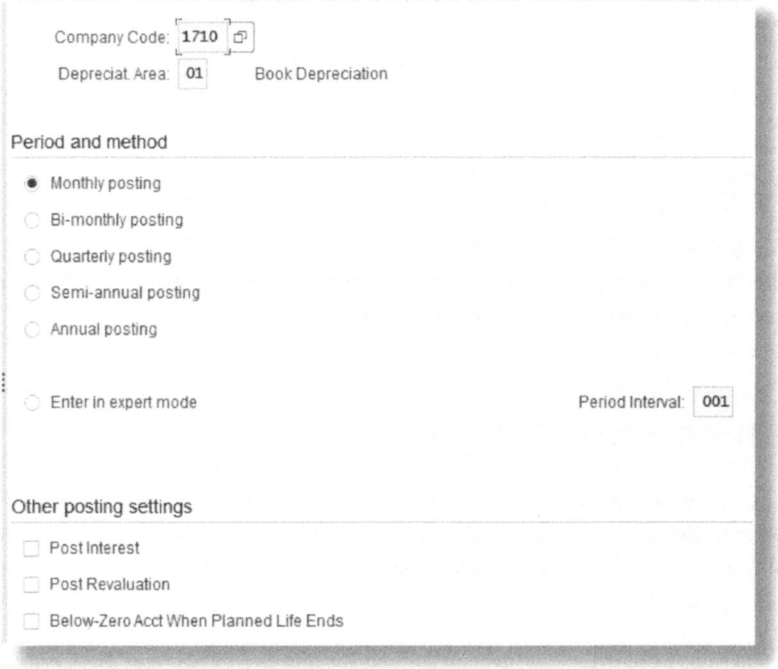

Company Code: **1710**

Depreciat. Area: **01**   Book Depreciation

Period and method

● Monthly posting
○ Bi-monthly posting
○ Quarterly posting
○ Semi-annual posting
○ Annual posting

○ Enter in expert mode   Period Interval: **001**

Other posting settings

☐ Post Interest
☐ Post Revaluation
☐ Below-Zero Acct When Planned Life Ends

Figure 3.18: Specify intervals and posting rules

3.9 Country specific

Some countries will have specific asset accounting requirements, and they can be found here. You will find Turkey and Russia nodes in the configuration to implement legal requirements compulsory for those countries. If you think you might have country-specific requirements, engage with your local consultant to find out more.

3.10 Segment reporting

Segment reporting can be activated in this section of the IMG, as shown in Figure 3.19. Once activated, it cannot be deactivated. Also, activating the functionality will result in the profit center field being displayed in the asset master record; the segment field can also be made to display its status. After activating, the fields will be blank, but there is also a node to populate the two fields via derivation, or population.

Figure 3.19: Segment reporting active

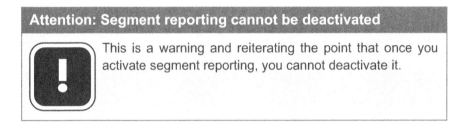

Attention: Segment reporting cannot be deactivated

This is a warning and reiterating the point that once you activate segment reporting, you cannot deactivate it.

3.11 Additional account assignment objects

Usually, the most common object for receiving monthly asset depreciation or amortization is the cost center. Alternatively, other *account assignment objects* can be used to collect depreciation, such as internal orders, and then be allocated across other objects or cost centers, for example. It is also possible to post depreciation to cost centers and then allocate the expense to other cost centers via controlling.

3.11.1 Activate account assignment objects

Figure 3.20 shows the different types of objects that can be used for account assignment, and whether an account assignment element is active or not.

< **SAP**	Change View "Account Assignment Elements for Asset Accounting": Overvi		

Undo Change   Select All   Select Block   Deselect All   More ∨

Account Assignment Elements for Asset Accounting

AcctAsgnOb	Account Assignment Object Name	Active	Bal. Sh...	Agree...
CAUFN	Internal Order	✓	☐	
EAUFN	Investment Order	✓		☐
FISTL	Funds Center	☐	✓	✓
FISTL2	Funds Center for Investment	☐	✓	✓
FKBER	Functional Area	✓	☐	☐
FKBER2	Functional Area for Investment	☐	✓	✓
GEBER	Fund	☐	✓	✓
GEBER2	Fund for Investment	☐	✓	✓
GRANT_NBR	Grant	☐	✓	✓
GRANT_NBR2	Grant for Cap. Investment	☐	✓	✓
IAUFN	Maintenance Order	✓	☐	
IMKEY	Real Estate Object	☐	☐	
KOSTL	Cost Center	✓	☐	✓
LSTAR	Activity Type	✓	☐	☐
PRCTR	Profit Center	✓	☐	✓
PS_PSP_PNR	WBS Element of Investment Project	✓		☐
PS_PSP_PN...	WBS Element	☐	☐	☐
SEGMENT	Segment	✓	☐	✓

Figure 3.20: Account assignment elements

3.11.2 Specify account assignment types for account assignment objects

After the objects are set to ACTIVE, then you can set up the depreciation area and company code combination to post to these objects. Figure 3.21 shows the INTERNAL ORDER, COST CENTER, and ACTIVITY TYPE are all set up for DEPRECIATION POSTINGS in the DEPRECIATION RUN, in addition to APC VALUES POSTINGS. These objects are only necessary for the depreciation areas that will be posting to the ledgers. In Figure 3.21, you can also see the objects that are specifically being used in the COMPANY CODE and DEPRECIATION AREA.

Figure 3.21: Account assignment objects

3.11.3 Process error table

When you set the agreement indicator in the account assignment object configuration, you need to configure the error message type in the process error table. The error message will be displayed when the object is compared to the next posting and found to be different than the master data record. See Figure 3.22.

AcctAsgnOb	AAObj.Name	Error	
CAUFN	Internal Order	No message	∨
EAUFN	Investment Order	No message	∨
FISTL	Funds Center	No message	∨
FISTL2	Funds Center for Investment	No message	∨
FKBER	Functional Area	Error message	∨
FKBER2	Functional Area for Investment	Error message	∨
GEBER	Fund	Error message	∨
GEBER2	Fund for Investment	Error message	∨
GRANT_NBR	Grant	Error message	∨
GRANT_NBR2	Grant for Cap. Investment	Error message	∨

Figure 3.22: Account assignment objects

3.11.4 Display of active account assignment objects

You can use the standard report option to display the active account assignment objects by company code. Choose your parameters and run the report to see the active account assignment objects. Please review Figure 3.23, to see the report selections for the active account assignment objects for your company code.

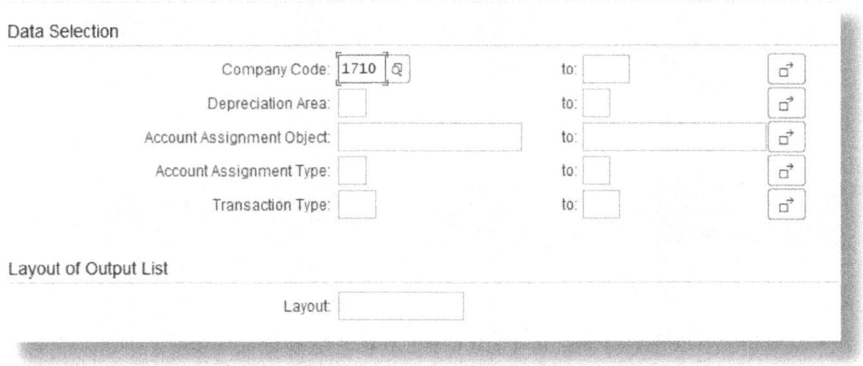

Data Selection

Company Code:	1710	Q	to:	
Depreciation Area:			to:	
Account Assignment Object:			to:	
Account Assignment Type:			to:	
Transaction Type:			to:	

Layout of Output List

Layout:

Figure 3.23: Display assignment objects by company code

4 General valuation

This section of the configuration reviews the valuation and depreciation areas that make up the chart of depreciation. It is very easy to consider the depreciation areas as the foundational building block for successful asset accounting, and thus implies a correctly configured chart of depreciation.

4.1 Set the chart of depreciation

Each time you enter the IMG for the first time, or log in to the SAP system, you will have to define the chart of depreciation you are working in, or making changes to, for the depreciation areas. The transaction code for this item is OAPL. If you are a company with only one country, and only have company codes in one country, you will probably never need this transaction. But, when you are making changes in the Canadian chart and also the US chart, then you will need to make sure that you use this transaction code to switch between the two charts of depreciation. You can see this change window in Figure 4.1.

Figure 4.1: Chart of depreciation selection

Naming conventions are important when using this transaction code, and in other areas of SAP Asset Accounting. Simply using numbers may be enough if you only have a few charts in your system, but if you have several countries in your system, then you may want to consider incorporating a country code in the name of the chart, like US01 for a US chart; CA01, for a Canadian chart, MX01 for a Mexican chart, etc. The naming is helpful in other configuration areas, and also helps the SAP Asset Accounting development team be more efficient in choosing the chart of depreciation that needs to be updated or changed down the road.

4.2 Depreciation areas

Generally, you will most likely not have to add any new depreciation areas to the chart of depreciation you use, but there are benefits to using the standard chart and copying it for your use with the company codes in your SAP system. Depreciation areas can be real or statistical. Real depreciation areas will post to a ledger or ledgers, and statistical areas will not post to ledgers as they are only for balance tracking in the asset ledger.

4.2.1 Define depreciation areas

Figure 4.2 shows where the depreciation areas are defined and where the *accounting principle* is assigned to each area.

Define Depreciation Areas

Ar.	Name of Depreciation Area	Real	Trgt Group	Acc.Princ.	G/L	
1	Book Depreciation	✓	2L	LG	Area Posts in Real Time	
2	Book Depreciation	✓	2L	LG	Area Does Not Post	
30	Local GAAP-local currency	✓	2L	LG	Area Does Not Post	
32	IFRS in local currency	✓	0L	IFRS	Area Posts in Real Time	
33	IFRS in group currency	✓	0L	IFRS	Area Does Not Post	
34	Local GAAP-Group currency	✓	2L	LG	Area Does Not Post	
90	Federal Tax ACRS/MACRS	✓	2L	LG	Area Does Not Post	
91	Alternative Minimum Tax	✓	2L	LG	Area Does Not Post	
92	Adjusted Current Earnings	✓	2L	LG	Area Does Not Post	
93	Corporate Earnings & Profits	✓	2L	LG	Area Does Not Post	

Figure 4.2: Define depreciation areas

When you define a depreciation area, you want to determine the name of the area, the accounting principle, and how the area posts to the General Ledger. When you choose AREA DOES NOT POST, you are essentially limiting this area to a statistical depreciation area, and usually that is all that is needed. You can still post transactional adjustments to these statistical areas, but the values stay in SAP Asset Accounting and do not go to other ledgers in SAP.

Areas that are not statistical, or 'real' areas, do post to the General Ledger, and are the heavy lifters in the Asset Accounting module. Typically, Area 01 will post to the General Ledger and in the leading ledger. Area 02, or another area that is so designated, can post to another ledger, the non-leading ledger, or local ledger. This local ledger will get values sourced from Area 01, and can manage its own set of postings. In one scenario, the local ledger may not need values, so the area may accept values from Area 01, and then based on the configuration, the values are negated or neutralized via ASKBN, or periodic postings. So, the two postings taken together, would net to zero for the ledger and the specific asset master record. If you have used SAP before SAP S/4HANA, then you will remember this is how ECC was designed to work. But in SAP S/4HANA, the posting is real-time and we can choose which depreciation areas get posted, at the time of posting.

Specifying the asset type is also done here, and then you can usually use the default value from the reference chart of depreciation. Only in special cases will you need to consider changing the default value for depreciation area; these are rare occurrences.

To summarize, the chart of depreciation gets assigned a company code. In the chart, you can have many depreciation areas, and each area can have a different *currency type* and currency. In addition, each area can have different depreciation keys, or different depreciation methods. The types of depreciation areas can differ widely, and a typical setup will contain local reporting for Depreciation Area 01, tax reporting in another depreciation area, parallel valuation in another depreciation area and in a separate currency, and even another depreciation area for group consolidation. It is possible you may need several depreciation areas, depending on how much a company wants to record in SAP, and benefit by the parallel ability to track a single asset master record, with so many different valuations.

4.2.2   Define depreciation areas for quantity update

In this section, you are turning on the tracking for quantity updates, and this is done by depreciation area. One example for using the depreciation-area-specific quantity tracking is for low-value assets. Keep in mind that you can also update quantity values on the asset master record, via transaction code AS02. Please review Figure 4.3 to see the updated quantity that is active for Depreciation Area 01.

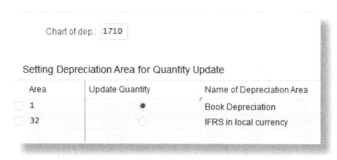

Figure 4.3: Define depreciation areas for quantity update

4.2.3 Specify transfer of APC (acquisition and production cost) values

Each depreciation area has a unique depreciation area that it copies its values from during the transaction update for the asset master record. The exception to this is Depreciation Area 01, which is the source for all the other areas, either directly or indirectly. For example, if you post an acquisition for an asset, depreciation will be posted in Area 01, and then based on the transaction type and the setting for the depreciation area, the next depreciation area may get a posting, too. So, ordinarily, with a plain vanilla acquisition posting, the cost of the acquisition will get posted to Area 01 identically, and all the subsequent areas that have Area 01 shown as the source will have the identical box checked.

For cost accounting reasons, there may be certain types of acquisitions you do not want to be identically copied over into the other areas used in the chart of depreciation. Please review Figure 4.4 to see where Area 01 is the source for other areas, and indirectly all areas.

Ar.	Name of Depreciation Area	ValAd	Ident.
01	Book Depreciation	00	
02	Book Depreciation	01	✓
30	Local GAAP-local currency	01	☐
32	IFRS in local currency	00	
33	IFRS in group currency	32	✓
34	Local GAAP-Group currency	01	✓
90	Federal Tax ACRS/MACRS	01	☐
91	Alternative Minimum Tax	90	✓
92	Adjusted Current Earnings	90	✓
93	Corporate Earnings & Profits	90	✓
94	Special Valuations	90	✓

Chart of dep.: **1710** Chart of Depreciation 1710 US

Figure 4.4: Specify transfer of acquisition and production cost (APC) values

4.2.4 Specify transfer of depreciation terms

As another example, if the area is used for tax depreciation, it would not be identical, and would get the acquisition posting value from Area 01, or another tax area, like Area 10, and may or may not have a specific percentage of the asset acquisition value reduced first, before posting the acquisition value to the depreciation area.

Figure 4.5 shows that Area 01 is the source of values for other areas, and indirectly, all areas. In some areas, the IDENTICAL box is checked, so that this is an identical copy, except for the difference in currency type.

45

Chart of dep.: 1110   Chart of Depreciation 1110 GB

Ar.	Name of Depreciation Area	TTr	Identical
01	Book Depreciation	00	
15	Local Tax in local currency	01	☐
31	Local GAAP in group currency	01	☑
32	IFRS in local currency	00	
33	IFRS in group currency	32	☑

Figure 4.5: Specify transfer of depreciation terms

4.2.5   Subsequent implementation of a depreciation area

Just in case the initial setup of the chart of depreciation is missing a depreciation area, SAP gives you a way out, or an ability to update the chart with a new area. This is a very important endeavor, and one that should be embarked upon in a very careful manner.

Attention: Adding a new Depreciation Area

 Before proceeding, it would be wise to have an experienced consultant on hand, or someone who has gone through this exercise previously. If this process is not done correctly, this can lead to very disastrous circumstances that may or may not be recoverable. It is also strongly recommended that this be done at least twice in a test environment, with multiple reviews by technical folks, and also reviewed and approved by the company's asset accountants. It is not a good idea to try to rush through this process. Please take your time when going through this exercise, and be sure to allow for extra time to review and analyze the results.

Now, after considering the aforementioned repeated warnings, adding a new depreciation area can provide a great benefit when you have a chart of depreciation that has been inadequately set up at the time of implementation. Or due to some unforeseen statutory requirement, or legal changes, it might be necessary to add a new area. Early on, implementations have a limited set of requirements, after that, things change, businesses grow, needs change, businesses are acquired or divested, and then you have needs that exist that did not at the original implementation.

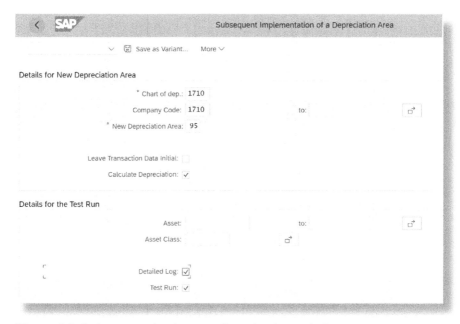

Figure 4.6: Subsequent implementation of a depreciation area

Please review Figure 4.6 to see that the chart of depreciation is selected, with COMPANY CODE and NEW DEPRECIATION AREA. Depending on what is necessary, or in scope for the new area, you may want to create the new area with no transaction data copied into the new area. So, if you don't want to copy previous adjustments or postings made to assets in the source area, be sure to select LEAVE TRANSACTION DETAIL INITIAL. Again, this just depends on what is needed in the new area. Also, the option to calculate depreciation is available and it will use the depreciation parameters that are assigned in the new area. It is also a good idea to run this job with the TEST RUN box checked.

4.2.6 Country-specific settings

In Russia, Ukraine, and Kazakhstan, it is sometimes necessary to change the length of the period for which the periodic depreciation is calculated. This option can be changed and configured with country-specific settings.

It is always a good idea to have a local consultant help with these changes and decisions.

4.3   Determine depreciation areas in the asset class

All asset classes are not equal, and here is where you can decide which depreciation areas are needed for an asset class. The transaction code for this configuration setting is OAYZ. One quick example, in the case of goodwill for a corporate entity where the goodwill exists in non-domestic entities, the goodwill may not be needed for local reporting ledgers. The depreciation areas can be deactivated for the non-domestic company, so that values are only tracked in Area 01, and not in the local ledger depreciation area, and no postings are needed in the local ledger and area.

Figure 4.7 shows that Area 94 is deactivated for ASSET CLASS 2000 in chart of depreciation 1710. So, this means that when you create assets in class 2000, for Chart 1710, Area 94 will not be included, and will not appear in the asset master record when you review values for the asset.

| Asset Class: 2000 | | | Machinery and Equipment | | | | |
| Chart of dep.: 1710 | | | Chart of Depreciation 1710 US | | | | |

Ar.	Dep. Area	Deact	DepKy	Use	Per	Index	Layou
01	Book Deprctn	☐	YSL1	10			2000
02	Book Deprctn	☐	LINA	12	0		2000
30	GAAP-local c	☐	LINA	12			2000
32	IFRS loc cur	☐	YSL1	8			2000
33	IFRS grp cur	☐	YSL1	8	0		2000
34	GAAP-Grp cur	☐	LINA	12	0		2000
90	ACRS/MACRS	☐	Y200	7			2000
91	ALT MIN	☐	Y150	7			2000
92	ACE	☐	Y150	7			2000
93	E&P	☐	YSL5	10			2000
94	SV	☑					2000

Figure 4.7: Depreciation areas in the asset class

4.4   Deactivate asset class for chart of depreciation

Deactivating the asset class will effectively cut off any assets being entered in this asset class in the chart of depreciation. All company codes set up with this chart of depreciation will not be allowed to create asset records in this asset class. Figure 4.8 shows that Asset Class 1000 is locked.

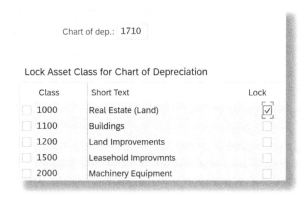

Figure 4.8: Lock asset class

4.5   Amount specifications for company code and depreciation areas

4.5.1   Specify maximum amount for low-value assets

In this section, you can set the low and maximum asset amounts for the LVA. The currencies are determined in another node, where the areas are assigned their currency code. You can also assign depreciation to check for the LVA amounts. Figure 4.9 shows Area 01 set up with a low-value asset amount of 500.00 USD.

Company Code: 1710   California Data Ltd

Ar.	Name of Depreciation Area	LVA Amount	MaxLVA Pur	Crcy
01	Book Depreciation	500.00	550.00	USD
02	Book Depreciation	500.00	550.00	EUR
30	Local GAAP-local currency	500.00	550.00	USD
32	IFRS in local currency	500.00	550.00	USD
33	IFRS in group currency	500.00	550.00	EUR
34	Local GAAP-Group currency	500.00	550.00	EUR
90	Federal Tax ACRS/MACRS	500.00	550.00	USD
91	Alternative Minimum Tax	500.00	550.00	USD
92	Adjusted Current Earnings	500.00	550.00	USD

Figure 4.9: Low-value asset amounts

In the second step of this configuration node, you can identify the asset class that will be a low-value asset class. Figure 4.10 shows that ASSET CLASS 5000 is active as a low-value asset.

Asset class	Asset Class Description
3210	Computer Software
4000	Assets under Construction
4001	AuC as Investment Measure
✓ 5000	Low-value Assets

Figure 4.10: Specify low-value asset class

4.5.2   Specify rounding of net book value and/or depreciation

These settings will vary from country to country due to legal and statutory reasons, but in this configuration node you can set up rounding for depreciation and net book value based on company code and depreciation area. The rounding will take place either at year end for net book value (NBV); or at period end in the case of calculated depreciation, and with three types of rounding available: arithmetic rounding, rounding up, and rounding down. Figure 4.11 shows that Area 01 is set up for ARITHMETIC ROUNDING.

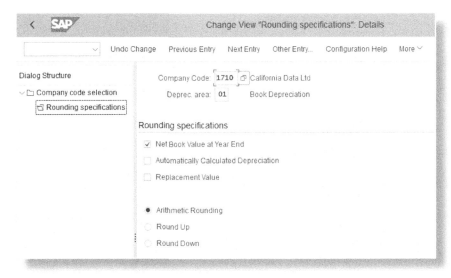

Figure 4.11: Specify rounding specifications

4.5.3   Specify changeover amount

This configuration node allows you to define the amount at which the depreciation calculation is assigned to the CHANGEOVER KEY in the depreciation key. Setting the *changeover amount* enables the calculations to diverge from the original calculation to the remaining value calculation. This is an optional configuration and can be left blank if no specific need is identified. Figure 4.12 shows that Area 01 and Area 02 are set up with changeover amounts of 1.00 USD and 1.00 EUR, respectively.

Figure 4.12: Specify changeover amount

4.5.4 Specify memo value

In the first option of this configuration node, you can set up the asset class so that it does not take the *memo value* into account, or is not active for the asset class. Figure 4.13 shows that Class 1100 is set up so that it does not take the memo value into account.

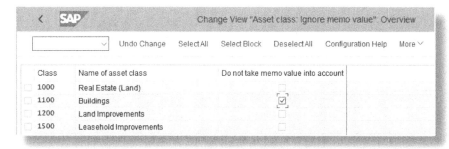

Figure 4.13: Specify ignore memo value

In the second option of this configuration node, you can specify the residual value that is not depreciated. The memo value is set up by amount in depreciation area and by company code. Figure 4.14 shows that Area 01 is set up with a memo value of 100.00 USD.

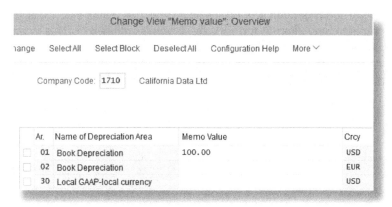

Figure 4.14: Specify memo value

In the last year of the asset's life, the memo value will not be depreciated, as shown in Figure 4.15.

Book Depreciation:2018 -2056

Fiscal year	Σ APC transactions	Acquisition value	Σ Ordinary deprec.	Net book value	Crcy
2047		17,299,934.00	432,499.00-	3,604,132.00	USD
2048		17,299,934.00	432,499.00-	3,171,633.00	USD
2049		17,299,934.00	432,499.00-	2,739,134.00	USD
2050		17,299,934.00	432,499.00-	2,306,635.00	USD
2051		17,299,934.00	432,499.00-	1,874,136.00	USD
2052		17,299,934.00	432,499.00-	1,441,637.00	USD
2053		17,299,934.00	432,499.00-	1,009,138.00	USD
2054		17,299,934.00	432,499.00-	576,639.00	USD
2055		17,299,934.00	432,499.00-	144,140.00	USD
2056		17,299,934.00	144,040.00-	100.00	USD
▪	17,299,934.00		▪ 17,299,834.00-		USD

Figure 4.15: Memo value is not depreciated

4.6 Fiscal year specifications

Normally, the fiscal year for a company code will be 12 periods and may potentially have four special periods, too. This is set up and configured in the Financial Accounting Global Settings configuration space. In the case of SAP Asset Accounting, often there is a need to have a 24-period year, and this fiscal year will be identified differently than the one in the company code configuration. The fiscal year is different from the G/L fiscal year and can be identified here.

4.6.1 Fiscal year variants

Specify other variants on company code level

In this node, you can specify the fiscal year variant that is different from the one specified in the global settings for the company code. Figure 4.16 shows where the fiscal year version can be assigned when it needs to be different from the one assigned in the company code.

53

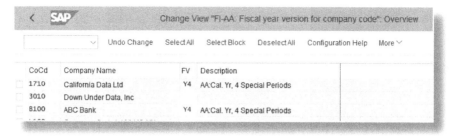

Figure 4.16: Specify fiscal year version for company code

Allow differing variants for depreciation areas with G/L integration

This is not a common configuration setting, but if the need to have different fiscal year variants for different depreciation areas that post to parallel ledgers exists, this functionality needs to be active. Figure 4.17 shows company code 1010 with a different fiscal year variant.

CoCd	Company Name	Diff. FY Variant
1010	Hamburg	☑
1011	Fair Trade Coffee GmbH	☐
1012	Fair Trade Coffee GmbH	☐

Alternative Fiscal Year Variants

Figure 4.17: Specify different fiscal year variant

Specify other variants on depreciation area level

In case you need to have the same fiscal year variant for the G/L and Area 01 for book depreciation, but another fiscal year variant for tax depreciation in a different depreciation area, you can make the determination here, in this configuration node. Figure 4.18 shows different fiscal year versions for Area 01 and Area 15.

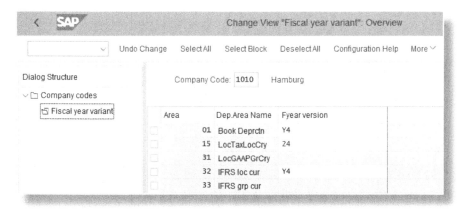

Figure 4.18: Assign different fiscal year variant in depreciation area

4.6.2 Shortened fiscal years

In the case of data migration, where you have a new fiscal year that is less than the normal 12 months, you can make adjustments for the fiscal year in this configuration section. Also, in the case where a company wants to change the fiscal year timing, this exercise may be needed. This may be necessary when a company changes from a 52-week calendar to a 12-month calendar, or vice versa, and depending upon the time of year the switch happens.

Define reduction rules for shortened fiscal years

If you need to reduce the depreciation for the shortened fiscal year, then you need to add the year and areas that need to have the reduction based on the shortened fiscal year. The system will then use the configuration and make the calculation adjustments. Figure 4.19 shows that REDUCTION RULES apply to Area 01 for fiscal year 2019.

Figure 4.19: Define reduction rules

Maintain depreciation key

Use this link or node to access the depreciation key to modify for reduction rules or shortened fiscal years.

4.6.3   Use of half months in the company code

It is possible to use a 24-period fiscal year for assets, with a 12-month fiscal year in the global settings for the company code. In this configuration node, determine the mid-month date, and save. Figure 4.20 shows the mid-month is 15 for company code 1010.

CoCd	Company Name	MidMon
1010	Hamburg	15

Figure 4.20: Use of half month in company code

4.6.4   Define weighting of periods

If periods need to have a different weight for depreciation calculations, the configuration can be made in this section. This is sometimes needed in a 4-4-5 calendar situation. An example where each of the first three periods would be unequally weighted, is shown in the next section.

Specify areas for individual period weighting

When you need depreciation posted unevenly, in the case of weeks in a 4-4-5 calendar year, this configuration will allow depreciation to be calculated based on weeks, and not post depreciation by 12 months of the year. Figure 4.21 shows that Area 01 is set up for a 4-4-5 calendar year.

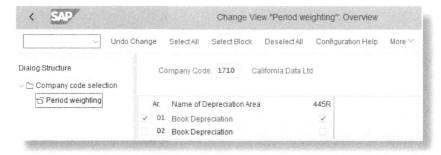

Figure 4.21: Assign 445 calendar year

4.7 Currencies

4.7.1 Define depreciation areas for foreign currencies

In this configuration node, you identify the currency code for the depreciation area, keeping in mind that BOOK DEPRECIATION in Area 01 is the company code currency. Figure 4.22 shows the currency assigned to each depreciation area.

Company Code: 1710   California Data Ltd

Ar.	Name of Depreciation Area	Crcy	Short text	ValAd	IdAPC
01	Book Depreciation	USD	US Dollar	0	
02	Book Depreciation	EUR	Euro	1	
30	Local GAAP-local currency	USD	US Dollar	1	
32	IFRS in local currency	USD	US Dollar	0	
33	IFRS in group currency	EUR	Euro	32	
34	Local GAAP-Group currency	EUR	Euro	1	
90	Federal Tax ACRS/MACRS	USD	US Dollar	1	
91	Alternative Minimum Tax	USD	US Dollar	90	
92	Adjusted Current Earnings	USD	US Dollar	90	
93	Corporate Earnings & Profits	USD	US Dollar	90	
94	Special Valuations	USD	US Dollar	90	

Figure 4.22: Define currency code in depreciation area

57

4.7.2 Specify the use of parallel currencies

These parallel currencies need to match up with the General Ledger, if the G/L also manages parallel currencies. Figure 4.23 shows the currency type assigned to the depreciation area.

Chart of dep.: 1710

Set Up Parallel Currencies

Ar.	Dep. Area	Currency Type		ValAd	IdAPC	TTr	IdntTrm
1	Book Deprctn		∨	0		0	
2	Book Deprctn		∨	1	✓	1	✓
30	GAAP-local c		∨	1		1	
32	IFRS loc cur		∨	0		0	
33	IFRS grp cur	Group Currency	∨	32	✓	32	✓
34	GAAP-Grp cur	Group Currency	∨	1	✓	1	✓
90	ACRS/MACRS		∨	1		0	
91	ALT MIN		∨	90	✓	0	
92	ACE		∨	90	✓	0	
93	E&P		∨	90	✓	0	
94	SV		∨	90	✓	0	

Figure 4.23: Define currency type in depreciation area

4.8 Group assets

4.8.1 Specify depreciation areas for group assets

If your company code is used to manage group assets, then the depreciation area needs to be active for group assets. Check the applicable box to activate group assets.

4.8.2 Specify asset classes for group assets

Additionally, if you want to set up an asset class that manages group assets, check the applicable box.

5 Depreciation

This chapter defines the different depreciation areas and how they are going to accept values when posting to asset master records. It also defines how the areas will accept and post the different types of depreciation: ordinary depreciation, special depreciation, unplanned depreciation, and manual depreciation. Additionally, it defines all of the depreciation parameters that will determine how the different depreciation types are calculated and by what methods they are calculated.

5.1 Ordinary depreciation

Ordinary depreciation is just that, your plain vanilla depreciation (or amortization) such as straight line or double-declining. This is the monthly or periodic depreciation that most assets have and post each period. Figure 5.1 shows all depreciation areas that are set up for ordinary depreciation.

Depr.area	Name of Depreciation Area	Ord. depr.
01	Book Depreciation	✓
02	Book Depreciation	✓
30	Local GAAP-local currency	✓
32	IFRS in local currency	✓
33	IFRS in group currency	✓
34	Local GAAP-Group currency	✓
90	Federal Tax ACRS/MACRS	✓
91	Alternative Minimum Tax	✓
92	Adjusted Current Earnings	✓
93	Corporate Earnings & Profits	✓
94	Special Valuations	✓

Figure 5.1: Depreciation areas with ordinary depreciation

5.1.1 Determine depreciation areas

In this section, you are defining which areas will post ordinary depreciation. Figure 5.2 shows that Area 01 is set up for Only negative values and zero allowed.

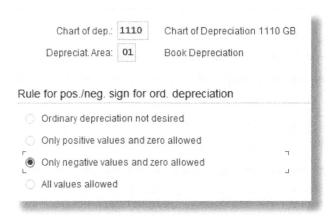

Figure 5.2: Specify ordinary depreciation

Furthermore, you can define if all values, positive, negative, or none is allowed, as shown in Figure 5.3.

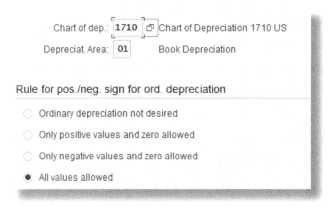

Figure 5.3: Specify values for ordinary depreciation

5.1.2   Assign accounts

This section is optional since you should have already defined these in the earlier nodes of the IMG, in section, 3.1.2 Assign G/L accounts. Figure 5.4 shows the G/L accounts assigned for ordinary depreciation.

Chart of Accts:	YCOA	Standard Chart of Accounts
Account Determ.:	160020	Machinery and Equipment
Deprec. area:	1	Book Depreciation

Ordinary depreciation account assignment

Acc.dep. accnt for ordinary depreciation:	17002000	Acc.Depr'n Mch & Equ
Expense account for ordinary depreciat.:	64002000	Mach.& Equ-Dep.Exp.
Revenue from write-up on ord.deprec.:	71010200	Gain from Write Up

Account assignment for revaluation on depreciation

Reval. accumulated ord. depreciation:	17002000	Acc.Depr'n Mch & Equ
Offsetting accnt: Reval. ordinary deprc.:	71015000	OffsetAcct Reval Dep

Figure 5.4: Specify accounts for ordinary depreciation

5.1.3   Define unit of production depreciation

This section is for setting up unit of production depreciation. Here you can set up depreciation by way of how many units are produced, and then depreciate based on the number of units from a total number of units. Think of a machine or asset that can make a total of 12 widgets in a year, and then the machine must be retired. If you estimate 1 widget per month, then the depreciation key may look like the one shown in Figure 5.5.

Figure 5.5: Specify unit of production depreciation

5.2 Special depreciation

Special depreciation is usually driven by legal or statutory reasons that will cause unique or non-standard depreciation transactions. One example of special depreciation is bonus depreciation in the US, or additional first-year depreciation. It was established by the Job Creation and Worker Assistance Act in 2002. This was a legal measure that was passed to spur investment and accelerate depreciation. One additional note, in 2017, US Congress doubled the depreciation rate for bonus calculations from 50% to 100% in the first year, for qualified property.

One example of bonus depreciation is a chain of dry-cleaning stores that may be waiting to invest in new equipment. With the bonus tax deprecia-tion, they could go forward with the capital investment and buy new equip-ment. Hypothetically, this new equipment could help them clean and press clothes faster, and thus make them more efficient, leading to cost savings. This new equipment would then be subject to accelerated depreciation, maybe 30% or 40% more in the very first year (prior to 2017), and 100% if purchased after 2017. Then normal tax depreciation would occur after that initial bonus depreciation, until the asset reaches a zero net book value. The benefit here is that the dry cleaner's chain can buy the new equipment and use the high tax depreciation in the first year to offset the potential income from the efficiency of the new equipment. On the contrary, if they are not allowed to take the bonus depreciation up front, and offset income, then they may delay the purchase of that equipment. The object of the law was to encourage investment, so the need to capture special depreciation arises, and this is how it can be done in SAP.

Please see the SAP OSS Note 1316999—Special Depreciation USA: The American Recovery Act 2009 for more information on this special depreciation and how a business can use the bonus depreciation in SAP to save income by offsetting tax depreciation.

5.2.1 Determine depreciation areas

In this section, determine and define which areas will have special depreciation. This is similar to the section in ordinary depreciation, but not all areas will have special depreciation. Usually, for US company codes, only tax areas will have special depreciation.

5.2.2 Calculate ordinary depreciation before special depreciation

This is a unique setting that allows for special depreciation to calculate before ordinary depreciation. So, if you go back to the bonus depreciation example, you will want to make sure that the depreciation area that is used for tracking bonus/special depreciation has this setting unchecked. You want to ensure that the special depreciation of 30% or 50%, is calculated first, and then any straight line or double declining depreciation calculation would happen second. Figure 5.6 shows that special depreciation will calculate first and ordinary depreciation second.

Chart of dep.: **1710** Chart of Depreciation 1710 US

Ar.	Name of Depreciation Area	O.dep. before sp.dep.
01	Book Depreciation	
02	Book Depreciation	
30	Local GAAP-local currency	
32	IFRS in local currency	
33	IFRS in group currency	
34	Local GAAP-Group currency	
90	Federal Tax ACRS/MACRS	☐
91	Alternative Minimum Tax	☐
92	Adjusted Current Earnings	☐
93	Corporate Earnings & Profits	
94	Special Valuations	☐

Figure 5.6: Ordinary depreciation before special depreciation

5.2.3 Assign accounts

If the depreciation area that records special depreciation also posts to ledger accounts, then enter the General Ledger accounts here, similar to what you have seen in the ordinary depreciation areas that allow for posting to ledgers.

5.3 Unplanned depreciation

Unplanned depreciation is just that, it happens when circumstances occur which cause the asset to need unplanned depreciation. Usually, unplanned depreciation is posted by way of a transaction type specifically designed to be recorded separately from ordinary and special depreciation. Consider the case of a car being accidentally driven into a tree, but the damage sustained is not great. The car can still be useful and operational, but the value of the car will immediately decrease, and should have unplanned depreciation recorded.

5.4 Determine depreciation areas

If you plan to post unplanned depreciation, then ensure the depreciation area has been checked, so that it will allow the unplanned depreciation. Please review Figure 5.7 to see the depreciation areas set up for unplanned depreciation.

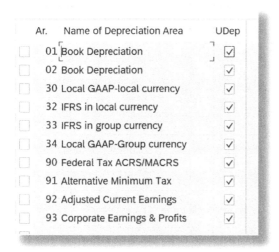

Ar.	Name of Depreciation Area	UDep
01	Book Depreciation	☑
02	Book Depreciation	☑
30	Local GAAP-local currency	☑
32	IFRS in local currency	☑
33	IFRS in group currency	☑
34	Local GAAP-Group currency	☑
90	Federal Tax ACRS/MACRS	☑
91	Alternative Minimum Tax	☑
92	Adjusted Current Earnings	☑
93	Corporate Earnings & Profits	☑

Figure 5.7: Unplanned depreciation

5.4.1   Assign accounts

Similar to posting unplanned depreciation to the same accounts as ordinary depreciation, you will not need separate accounts, since the ordinary and unplanned depreciation can be determined via standard asset accounting reports. If you need to have ordinary and unplanned depreciation posted to different accounts for legal or statutory reasons, be sure to identify the different accounts and enter them here.

5.4.2   Define transaction types for unplanned depreciation

If you need special transaction types for unplanned depreciation, then copy the standard types delivered by SAP and use a prefix of Y or Z. If not, then use the standard SAP transaction types. Keep in mind that transaction types specific to tax areas will need to be limited to those areas. This is covered in a later section, Chapter 8 Transactions. Figure 5.8, shows several transaction types set up for unplanned depreciation.

Transact. type	Transaction Type Name
620	Manual spec. dep. on prior-yr acquis per dep. key
630	Manual spec. dep. on curr-yr acquis per dep. key
640	Unplanned depreciation on prior-year acquisitions
641	Unplanned book depreciation on prior-yr acquis.
642	Unplanned tax depreciation on prior-yr acquis.
643	Unplanned group depreciation on prior-yr acquis.
650	Unplanned depreciation on current-yr acquisition
651	Unplanned book depreciation on current-yr acquis.
652	Unplanned tax depreciation on current-yr acquis.
653	Unplanned group depreciation on current-yr acquis.

Figure 5.8: Transaction types for unplanned depreciation

5.5   Valuation methods

Depreciation calculation in the FI-AA system is very flexible and is based on a dynamic way of using depreciation keys to define the calculation. Therefore, it is possible to represent many different depreciation methods using defined depreciation keys and calculation methods.

65

Standard depreciation keys and calculation methods for the most common types of depreciation are supplied in the system. They can be found in the different charts of depreciation by country. In the following sections, you can define your own depreciation keys and calculation methods for the automatic calculation of depreciation.

5.5.1 Depreciation key

Depreciation keys are where the magic happens. It is kind of like the kingdom of magic where a mouse and his mistress run around and play.

Calculation methods

In the following sections, you will define the calculation methods that are assigned to our depreciation keys. Most of the necessary methods are supplied by SAP; you should very rarely need to modify or update these methods.

▶   **Define base methods**

The base method is assigned to the depreciation key and is used to define what type of depreciation is posted, how the method is calculated, and the treatment of the asset after the end of depreciation. Figure 5.9 shows base method 0012 set for ordinary depreciation type.

Base Method:	0012	Ordinary: explicit percentage
* Type of Depreciation:		Ord.depreciation
*Dep. Method:		Stated percentage
Reduce Use.Life at FY End:		☐

Treatment of end of depreciation

Dep. After Pind.Life End:	No
Dep.Below NBValue Zero:	No
Curb:	No

Figure 5.9: Base methods for depreciation

▶ **Define declining balance methods**

The declining balance methods are defined for calculating declining depreciation. The double-declining balance for use in US tax depreciation, or method 004, is shown in Figure 5.10.

Chart of dep.: 1710   Chart of Depreciation 1710 US

Decl.-Bal.	Description of the Method	Dec.Factor	Max.Perc.	Min.Perc.
001	0.00x / 0.0000% / 0.0000%			
003	1.50x / 0.0000% / 0.0000%	1.50		
004	2.00x / 0.0000% / 0.0000%	2.00		
005	1.50x / 42.0000% / 0.0000%	1.50	42.0000	

Figure 5.10: Declining balance methods for depreciation

▶ **Define maximum amount methods**

The maximum amount method allows you to modify or limit the maximum amount for depreciation for a specified time frame, and is shown in Figure 5.11.

Maximum Amount: Y01

Description: Luxury Automobile Limits

Maximum Amounts

Valid To	Currency	Max.amount
31.12.2016	USD	3,160.00

Figure 5.11: Maximum amount methods for depreciation

▶ **Define multilevel method**

The multilevel method can be adjusted to handle bonus depreciation and set up the reduction of the asset value in the first year of acquisition, as shown in Figure 5.12. The multilevel method shown in Figure 5.12 shows a 50% reduction in each of the years 2015, 2016, and 2017, but up to 100% in the year 2018.

| Chart of dep.: | 1710 | Chart of Depreciation 1710 US |
| Multilev.Meth.: | Y01 | Bonus Depreciation |

Acq.Year	Years	Per	BaseVal.	Percent	Rem. Life	Reduct.
2015	0	1	01	0.0000		50.0000
2016	0	1	01	0.0000		50.0000
2017	0	1	01	0.0000		50.0000
2018	1	1	01	0.0000		100.0000|

Figure 5.12: Multilevel methods for depreciation

▶ **Maintain period control method**

One of the least understood areas of depreciation keys is the period control method. The period control method determines when a depreciation key starts depreciation at time of acquisition, when it starts for additional acquisitions, when it stops for retirements, and when it stops for transfers. Pay close attention to the settings of the period control in order to determine when the depreciation calculation is starting and stopping at time of transaction posting. Figure 5.13 shows Method 006 with the period control set to MID PERIOD for the four transaction groups.

Period Control

Prd.C.Meth	Description	Acq	Add	Ret	Trn
001	Period Start Date, Mid Date	01	01	02	02
003	Period Start, Start of Yr, Mid Date	01	06	02	02
004	Mid Year	07	06	07	07
006	Mid Period	03	03	03	03

Figure 5.13: Period control methods for depreciation

Default values

In this section, you can propose values for depreciation areas and company codes. You can propose these values by company code, depreciation area, and depreciation key with an effect on the interest key. Also, you can propose acquisition only in capitalization year for company codes.

Maintain depreciation key

Maintain depreciation key can be accessed via transaction code AFAMA; it is one of the most important transactions for all of the asset accounting configurations. This is where it all comes together for the depreciation key, and to manage depreciation for the asset and depreciation areas. Figure 5.14 shows key 0000—NO DEPRECIATION AND NO INTEREST, and it is assigned BASE METHOD 0002, for ordinary depreciation and no calculation. This unique depreciation key, 0000, does not calculate depreciation for the asset it is assigned to or the associated depreciation area.

Chart of dep.:	1710	Chart of Depreciation 1710 US
Dep. key:	0000	No depreciation and no interest

DepType:	Ord.depreciation
Phase:	From the start of depreciation

Assignment of Calculation Methods

*Base Method:	0002	Ordinary: no automatic depreciation
Decl.-bal. method:	001	0.00x / 0.0000% / 0.0000%
*Prd Cont:	001	
*Multilev.Meth.:	001	Base: NBV over remaining life

Class:	No assignment

Chnge. Method:	
Changeover%Rate:	

Multiple shift:	Increase in depreciation and expired useful life
Scrap Value:	Consideration is controlled by cutoff value key

Shutdown:	No

Figure 5.14: Maintain depreciation key

Period control

Period control is an important thing to be aware of, but hopefully no changes are needed in this configuration item.

▶ **Maintain period control**

The period control determines the date on which depreciation starts, in combination with the asset value date.

Some of the standard options available include:

- ▶ 01 Pro rata at period start date
- ▶ 02 Pro rata up to mid-period at period start date
- ▶ 03 Pro rata at mid-period
- ▶ 04 First year convention at half year start date
- ▶ 05 Year start date/Mid-year/Year-end (Austria)
- ▶ 06 At the start of the year
- ▶ 07 At mid-year
- ▶ 08 At the end of the year (=Start date of following year)
- ▶ 09 At mid-quarter
- ▶ 10 At the first quarter
- ▶ 11 Next month
- ▶ 12 Next quarter
- ▶ 13 Next half-year
- ▶ 14 Modified half-year rule
- ▶ 15 First-year convention at retirement (Korea)
- ▶ 16 First day same month, second till last day, next month (MX)
- ▶ 17 Current month (US, half months)

▶ **Define calendar assignments**

Once the period control is established, you must identify how the date is chosen for the specific period control. One special note for the calendar assignments is that for a 24-period year, the first period is zero, or 0, and the last period is 23. Or for a 12-period year, the first period is 0 and the 12th period is 11. Pay close attention to how the standard settings are delivered, and don't change them. Copy a prior fiscal year if you need to modify it and make the adjustments accordingly.

Figure 5.15 shows all of the items in the list for period control 02. Notice that the first item starts with a blank or zero in the period field, and the next two items are assigned 1 for the period. Any posting to the asset that is January 15th or earlier will fall in Period 0 (or the first calendar month). Likewise, any posting that is February 15th, or earlier, but later than January 15th will fall in Period 1 (or the second calendar month).

FV	Per.C...	Name for Period Control	Year	Mo	Dy	Period	MidMonth
K4	02	Pro rata upto mid-period at period start date		1	15		
K4	02	Pro rata upto mid-period at period start date		2	14	1	
K4	02	Pro rata upto mid-period at period start date		2	15	1	
K4	02	Pro rata upto mid-period at period start date		3	15	2	
K4	02	Pro rata upto mid-period at period start date		4	15	3	
K4	02	Pro rata upto mid-period at period start date		5	15	4	
K4	02	Pro rata upto mid-period at period start date		6	15	5	
K4	02	Pro rata upto mid-period at period start date		7	15	6	
K4	02	Pro rata upto mid-period at period start date		8	15	7	
K4	02	Pro rata upto mid-period at period start date		9	15	8	
K4	02	Pro rata upto mid-period at period start date		10	15	9	
K4	02	Pro rata upto mid-period at period start date		11	15	10	
K4	02	Pro rata upto mid-period at period start date		12	15	11	
K4	02	Pro rata upto mid-period at period start date		12	31	12	
K4	03	Pro rata at mid-period		1	31	1	✓
K4	03	Pro rata at mid-period		2	29	2	✓
K4	03	Pro rata at mid-period		3	31	3	✓

Figure 5.15: Define calendar assignments for period control

▶ **Define time-dependent period controls**

In this section, you can define the period control to be time dependent or based on the fiscal year. This is not common, but in some countries can be a statutory requirement.

In the first part of this configuration node, and shown in Figure 5.16, this depreciation key is assigned the configuration item PERIOD CONTROL ACCORDING TO FISCAL YEARS. This must be selected to allow for the time-dependent functionality to work with the depreciation key.

Chart of dep.:	1710
Description:	Chart of Depreciation 1710 US
Dep. key:	LINS	Str.-line over rem.life pro rata to zero
Status:	Active

| Maximum Amount: | |
| Cutoff Val. Key: | |

No Ordinary Dep. with Special Dep.: ☐
No Interest If No Deprec. Is Planned: ☐
Period control according to fiscal years: ☑
Dep. to the Day: ☐
No reduct. in short year: ☐

Figure 5.16: Define time-dependent period control in key

In the second part of this configuration node, you can assign the TIME-DEPENDENT PERIOD CONTROL for the depreciation key, and what fiscal year the time dependency is valid to, or when it will end. Figure 5.17 shows time dependency is set for acquisitions, and up to fiscal year 2020.

Company Code: 1710 California Data Ltd
Dep. key: YSL1 SL Current Month

Time-Dependent Period Control

To	Acq	Add	Ret	Trn	Rev.	InvS	UpDp	WUpR
2020	Y1							

Figure 5.17: Define time-dependent period control in depreciation key

▶ **Generate period controls**

Generating period controls is optional; it only needs to be performed if there is a year-dependent fiscal year. If so, you need to ensure this step is done each year, before the next fiscal year starts, and after the fiscal year dates have been entered in the Financial Accounting Global Settings. Figure 5.18 shows the settings for running the program for fiscal year K4 in year 2020.

Figure 5.18: Generate period control

After the program runs, the test results will be shown. In this case, the year is not populated because the fiscal year variant K4 is not set up for year dependency. See Figure 5.19.

Fiscal year variant: K4 Calendar year: 2020

Per.Con	Name for Period Control	Year	Mo	Dy	Period	MidMonth
02	Pro rata upto mid-period at period start date		1	15	000	
02	Pro rata upto mid-period at period start date		2	15	001	
02	Pro rata upto mid-period at period start date		3	15	002	

Figure 5.19: Generate period control results

5.5.2 Further settings

Some additional settings are available to adjust the depreciation calculations; they are cutoff value key, maximum base value, and base value percentages.

Cutoff value key

The cutoff value key can also be considered the scrap value key. Figure 5.20 shows key CL1 is given a description that implies a 10% scrap value, or cutoff.

Cutoff Value Keys

Cutoff Val	Name for Cutoff Value Key
☐ CL1	Cutoff value for Chile 10%
☐ CN1	Cutoff value for China 5%
☐ ICK	Cutoff value for India 5%
☐ JPS	Cutoff value for Japanese net worth tax dep.
☐ KR1	Cutoff value for Korea 10%, purchase prior 1/1/95
☐ KR2	Cutoff value for Korea 5%, decl.-balance assets
☐ SCH	Scrap value 10 %
☐ VRA	Cutoff value net worth tax Austria
☐ VRM	Cutoff value net worth tax Germany
☐	

Figure 5.20: Cutoff value keys

Figure 5.21 shows the cutoff value key is set up for 10% of the asset value, and this is where and when the depreciation is stopped from calculation.

Dialog Structure
∨☐ Cutoff Value Keys
  ☐ Levels

Cutoff Val. Key: **CL1**   Cutoff value for Chile 10%

Levels

	Valid To	To year of acq.	Validity in Yrs	Months Valid	CutoffPerc
☐	9999	9999	999	12	10,000
☐					

Figure 5.21: Assign cutoff value key percentage

Define maximum base value

Figure 5.22 shows where you identify and configure by company code, asset class, depreciation area, and the maximum base value. SAP will not depreciate more than the maximum, and if the actual cost or acquisition is less than the maximum, SAP will use the actual value.

	Company code	Asset class	Depr.area	Valid To	Maximum value
☐	1710	3100	90	31.12.2016	15.800,00
☐	1710	3100	90	31.12.2017	15.800,00
☐	1710	3100	91	31.12.2016	15.800,00
☐	1710	3100	91	31.12.2017	15.800,00
	1710	3100	92	31.12.2016	15.800,00

Figure 5.22: Define maximum base value

74

Specify asset-specific base value percentages

In this section, you can identify a company-code-specific asset, and assign a percentage for a specific time frame to reduce the base value for calculation of depreciation for the specified asset. After the time frame has expired, the full value of the asset is considered for the base value calculation.

5.5.3 Enhancements

At this point, if any of the depreciation settings mentioned so far are not capable of calculating your depreciation, SAP provides the ability to calculate with modifications via enhancement. One standard disclaimer here, if you need to enhance, be sure to bring in an experienced consultant to work with your ABAP developer, to ensure accuracy, and so you don't have unintended circumstances or results. Always be sure to thoroughly test the developed enhancement.

6 Special valuations

In this chapter, you will set up the configuration for special valuations on assets, special depreciation reserves, and special value adjustments. The special valuations section is dependent upon the configuration made in the general valuation area, where you create the definition of the depreciation area.

In order to set up a depreciation area for revaluation, the area to allow for revaluation values had to be defined when the depreciation area was defined; as shown in Chapter 4 General valuation. If the configuration for the depreciation area is not set correctly, then changes can't be made, since the options will not be available in the configuration nodes.

6.1 Special reserves

In the special reserves section, you will determine whether the system will post a write-off for a gross or net allocation. SAP recommends using the net posting method since this is in line with most statutory requirements. Once the decision is made to use net, then you will need to assign accounts for posting in the account determination.

6.1.1 Specify gross or net procedure

In this section, you define the gross or net procedure for write off of values against the asset by depreciation area.

6.1.2 Assign accounts

If you have special reserves, it is similar to other nodes in SAP Asset Accounting where you have assigned the G/L accounts for posting.

6.2 Transferred reserves

The transferred reserves section enables you to set up for transfer or reserves for tax depreciation purposes and to use the reserves to offset future acquisitions that are replacements for assets sold. The section allows you to choose which depreciation area will have transfer of reserves possible, and then update the depreciation area with the accounts that will be posted with the reserve values. Each posting will require an asset transaction type. This most likely will not be necessary because several standard transactions are delivered by SAP.

6.2.1 Determine depreciation areas

In the first step, define which depreciation areas are going to post transferred reserves, as shown in Figure 6.1.

Figure 6.1: Determine area for special reserves

6.2.2 Assign accounts

Next, assign the accounts that will be posted to for the reserves. This is only necessary if the area will be posting to a ledger. Select ACCOUNT DETERMINATION and enter the accounts, as depicted in Figure 6.2.

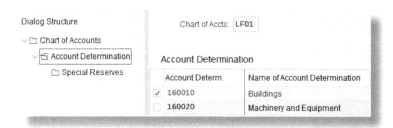

Figure 6.2: Assign accounts for special reserves

6.2.3 Define transaction types for transfer of reserves

SAP has provided standard transaction types for handling the reserves posting. Remember, this is for posting to assets, and these may or may not be posting to other ledgers external to SAP Asset Accounting. Ensure the transaction types are set up appropriately, as shown in Figure 6.3.

Transact. type	Transaction Type Name
500	Post depreciation
501	Scheduled Depreciation
502	Unplanned depreciation
503	Revaluation APC
504	Revaluation of accumulated depreciation
680	Transfer of reserves to prior-year acquisitions
682	Transfer of rsrvs to prior-yr acquis/ tax bal.sht.
690	Transfer of reserves to curr-yr acquis.
692	Transfer of reserves to acquisition/tax bal.sheet

Figure 6.3: Transaction types for transfer of reserves

6.3 Investment support

In the investment support section, the configuration is available to set up assets so that any type of special investment support, or grant, can be depreciated or amortized separately from the original asset acquisition costs.

First, you will need to determine which areas will have investment support and check the box for that depreciation area. Then, you will set up the investment support measure, and provide supplemental parameters for that investment measure.

6.3.1 Determine depreciation areas

As you have done in other configuration nodes, please make sure the areas are updated here for investment support, as shown in Figure 6.4.

Ar.	Name of Depreciation Area	Inv
01	Book Depreciation	✓
15	Local Tax in local currency	✓
31	Local GAAP in group currency	✓
32	IFRS in local currency	☐
33	IFRS in group currency	☐

Figure 6.4: Determine depreciation area for investment support

6.3.2 Define investment support measures

After setting up the investment support, determine the supporting characteristics. As needed, update the depreciation area for acquisition and production cost (APC) reduction, the time-dependent data, and the default values and check specifications, as shown in Figure 6.5.

Chart of dep.: 3010   Chart of Depreciation 3010 AU

Invest.Support: 01   IS TEST

Support Area: 15   Local Tax in local currency
Inv.Supp. Type: Asset reducti... ⌄

Specifications for check when claiming / retiring

Valid From: 01.01.2018   Valid To: 31.12.2020
Max.perc.rate: 10.0000   Max. Amount: 0.00
Base Area: 1   Book Depreciation
Retention Per.: 1 / 0
Per. from: From capitalization date   ⌄
Check specs.: No ⌄
Repayment type for premature retirement: Investment support is paid back completely

Substantiation for application

✓ Line Items
  Catch-Up

Figure 6.5: Define investment support measure

Define the areas for acquisition and production cost reduction, as shown in Figure 6.6.

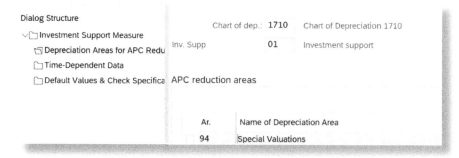

Figure 6.6: Define areas for investment support

Enter time-dependent validity dates from starting date to finishing date, as shown in Figure 6.7.

Figure 6.7: Define time-dependent investment support

Set up default values and checks, as shown in Figure 6.8.

Figure 6.8: Default values for investment support

6.3.3 Assign accounts

Again, if the depreciation area is posting to ledgers, you need to add the accounts here, similar to the other nodes where you assigned General Ledger accounts. Please review Figure 6.9 to see the accounts assigned for investment support.

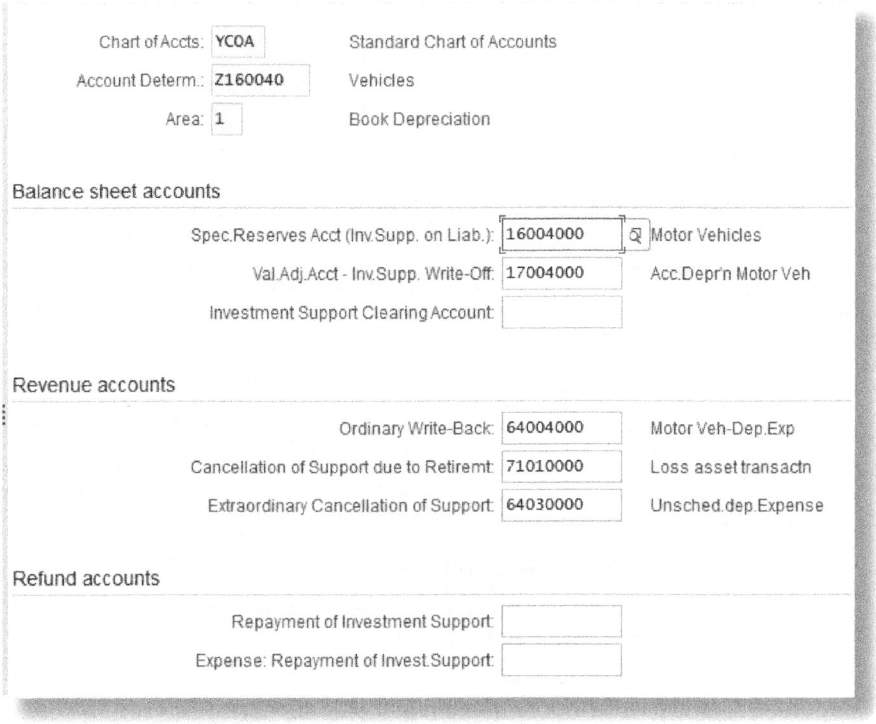

Figure 6.9: Assign accounts for investment support

6.3.4 Check transaction types for investment support

Where necessary, set up transaction types. Or, just use the ones delivered by SAP. Some transaction types delivered by SAP are shown in Figure 6.10.

Transact. type	Transaction Type Name
I00	Sample: D O N O T delete
I01	Investments in State sponsored area (liab. side)
IAA	Transaction type for invest. support measure AA
IBB	Transaction type for invest. support measure BB

Figure 6.10: Define transaction types for investment support

Limit transaction types to depreciation areas

You should not need to limit the posting to a specific area only in SAP S/4HANA. This type of configuration was needed in an earlier version of SAP. If it was configured, then you will see it in the LIMIT TRANSACTION TYPES TO DEPRECIATION AREAS section in the configuration. In Figure 6.11, you see an old transaction type set up for posting only in Area 15. This change in how SAP handles the new postings will be covered in more detail in Chapter 8 Transactions.

Chart of dep.: **3010**   Chart of Depreciation 3010 AU

Trans. Type: **I01**   Investments in State sponsored area (liab. side)

Ar.	Dep. Area
15	LocTaxLocCry

Figure 6.11: Limit transaction types for investment support

Limiting transaction types is no longer required

You should not have to limit any transaction types in SAP S/4HANA, as this is no longer required. The limitation of values in areas is done at the time of posting, and via selection of the ledgers and depreciation areas. This is a legacy configuration item, in case transaction types are brought over during migration.

Similar to the special reserves section, if there will be postings for investment support measures you will need to update the depreciation areas with accounts. If this is not possible, then you will find an informational message, as shown in Figure 6.12, stating "No entries for account assignment possible."

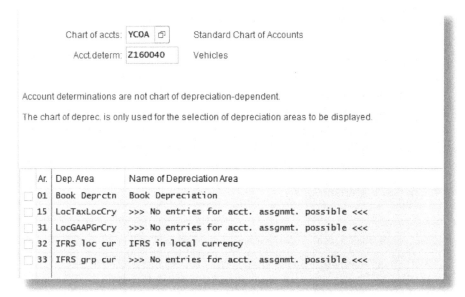

Figure 6.12: Update accounts for investment support by area

6.4 Revaluation of fixed assets

SAP allows for the revaluation of fixed assets to help track replacement values, and these replacement values are derived from the use of index values to calculate the revaluation postings.

6.4.1 Maintain accounts for revaluation

If the revaluation of assets is configured, you also need to set up the account determination to have accounts for the revaluation postings, as shown in Figure 6.13.

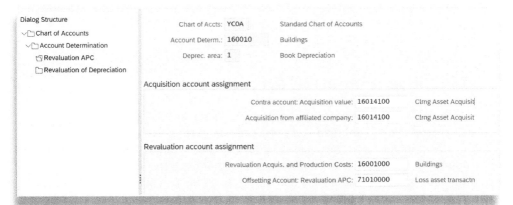

Figure 6.13: Update accounts for revaluation on acquisitions

Additionally, if revaluation of depreciation is to be configured, then the accounts need to be added in the account determination for the depreciation area for the revaluation postings, as shown in Figure 6.14.

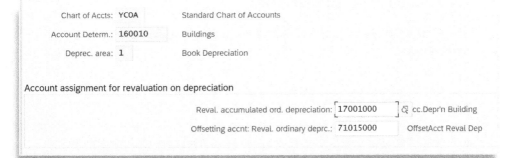

Figure 6.14: Update accounts for revaluation on depreciation

6.4.2 Indexed replacement values

Next, if the revaluation is configured, then you will need to determine which depreciation areas will have revaluation postings based on indexed replacement values. Next, define an index series that can be used in the calculation of the revaluation.

85

Lastly, assign the index series to the asset classes that will use the calculated values for the revaluation postings.

6.4.3 Revaluation for the balance sheet

SAP also allows for a different type of revaluation for the balance sheet, with respect to a one-time need or for periodic postings that may be needed to reflect inflationary type values. Both of these types of postings can be entered in the asset accounting module, either via transaction code ABAW Post Revaluation, ABAWN Post New Valuation, or via periodic posting, transaction code AR29N—Post Revaluation and New Valuation. Inflation can be posted periodically with transaction code J1AI—Inflation. You need to set up specific transaction types to handle the revaluation postings. Remember to use the standard SAP transaction types and limit the posting to the required depreciation areas during posting of values.

6.4.4 Country-specific functions

See your local consultant for help with country-specific settings and statutory needs.

6.5 Interest

In this section, you will define which areas are available for posting interest. Setting up the interest section is much like the revaluation section. You need to identify the depreciation areas for interest postings by checking the box in the configuration. Next, update the account determination with the accounts that will receive the interest postings. Interest postings are calculated during the depreciation posting program, which is transaction code AFAB.

6.5.1 Determine depreciation areas

Figure 6.15 shows Area 93 marked for interest postings.

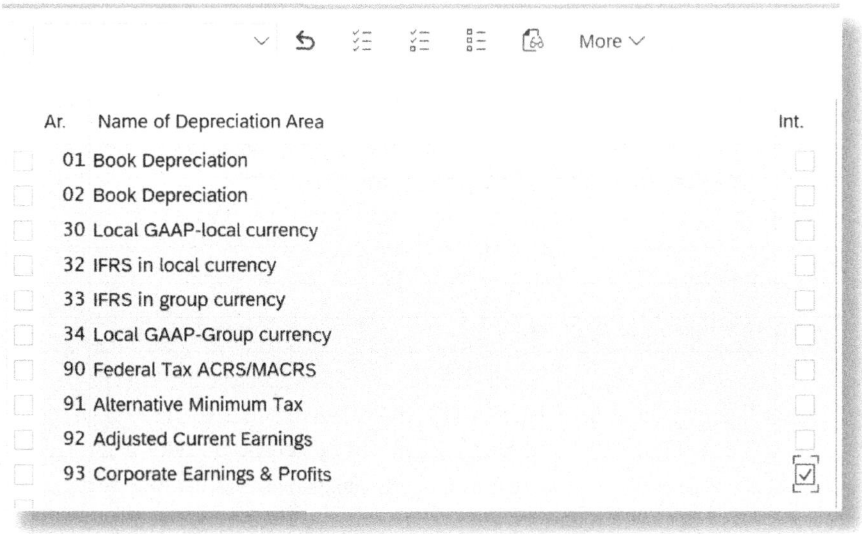

Ar.	Name of Depreciation Area	Int.
	01 Book Depreciation	
	02 Book Depreciation	
	30 Local GAAP-local currency	
	32 IFRS in local currency	
	33 IFRS in group currency	
	34 Local GAAP-Group currency	
	90 Federal Tax ACRS/MACRS	
	91 Alternative Minimum Tax	
	92 Adjusted Current Earnings	
	93 Corporate Earnings & Profits	☑

Figure 6.15: Determine depreciation areas for interest

6.5.2 Assign accounts

Again, if the area will post to the ledgers make sure to enter the General Ledger accounts in this section.

6.5.3 Maintain depreciation key

Then, lastly, update the depreciation key that will be assigned to the asset depreciation area to accept interest postings. Figure 6.16 shows the BASE METHOD 0029 is used for INTEREST: EXPLICIT PERCENTAGE.

Assignment of Calculation Methods

* Base Method:	0029	Interest: explicit percentage
Decl.-bal. method:	001	0.00x / 0.0000% / 0.0000%
* Prd Cont:	008	
* Multilev.Meth.:	052	Base: replacement value

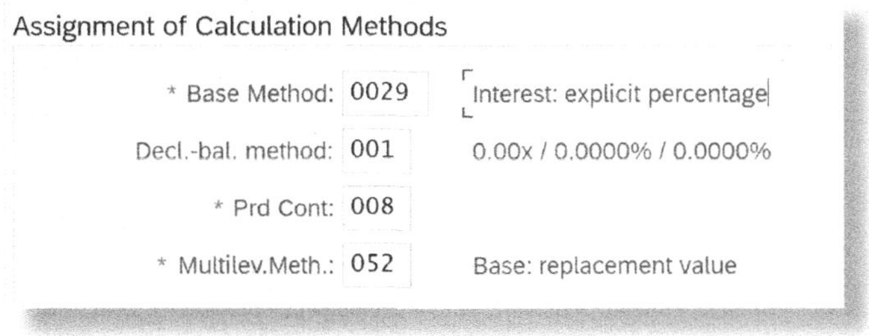

Figure 6.16: Maintain depreciation key for interest

The assignment of the base method to the depreciation key can be done in transaction code AFAMA. Although, to create more base methods, use transaction code AFAMP to update the list of base methods, which can then be used in creation or updates to existing depreciation keys for interest. Figure 6.17 shows the standard base methods for calculating interest; also found in transaction code AFAMP.

Base Method

Base Method	Text
○ 0028	Interest: leasing
○ 0029	Interest: explicit percentage
○ 0030	Interest: explicit percentage (after end of life)
○ 0031	Interest: explicit percentage (below zero)

Figure 6.17: Base methods for interest

6.6 Net worth tax

In this section, you define the setup for net worth tax.

6.6.1 Specify depreciation area

Identify the net worth tax depreciation area, company code, and chart of depreciation. An example for company code 1710 is shown in Figure 6.18.

FI-AA: Net worth area for company code

CoCd	Company Name	Property	Name of Depreciation Area	ChDep
☑ 1710	California Data Ltd	32	IFRS in local currency	1710
☐ 3010	Down Under Data, Inc	1	Book Depreciation	3010

Figure 6.18: Determine depreciation areas for net worth tax

6.6.2 Create property classification key

Identify the property class key, as shown in Figure 6.19.

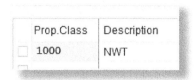

Figure 6.19: Determine property class for net worth tax

6.6.3 Create property indicator

Identify and create the net worth tax (NWT) property indicator, as shown in Figure 6.20.

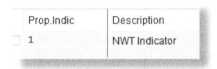

Figure 6.20: Create property indicator for net worth tax

6.6.4 Create reasons for manual depreciation

Identify and create the reasons for manual depreciation, as shown in Figure 6.21.

Figure 6.21: Create reasons for net worth tax

6.6.5 Define sort versions for net worth reports

Create the sort version, if needed, for the net worth tax reporting. If you don't like the standard options, then copy one and adjust to your needs; an example is shown in Figure 6.22.

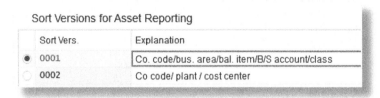

Sort Versions for Asset Reporting

	Sort Vers.	Explanation
●	0001	Co. code/bus. area/bal. item/B/S account/class
○	0002	Co code/ plant / cost center

Figure 6.22: Define sort versions for net worth tax

6.6.6 Depreciation key

Define the cutoff value key

Update your net worth tax depreciation key with the cutoff value key and define a new depreciation key if necessary. Also, update the index series, screen layouts, and asset classes as needed. A list of cutoff keys is shown in Figure 6.23.

Cutoff Value Keys

	Cutoff Val	Name for Cutoff Value Key
☐	CL1	Cutoff value for Chile 10%
☐	CN1	Cutoff value for China 5%
☐	ICK	Cutoff value for India 5%
☐	JPS	Cutoff value for Japanese net worth tax dep.
☐	KR1	Cutoff value for Korea 10%, purchase prior 1/1/95
☐	KR2	Cutoff value for Korea 5%, decl.-balance assets
☐	SCH	Scrap value 10 %
☐	VRA	Cutoff value net worth tax Austria
☐	VRM	Cutoff value net worth tax Germany

Figure 6.23: Define cutoff value keys

Next, assign the cutoff value key percentage, as shown in Figure 6.24.

Figure 6.24: Define cutoff value key percentage

Define depreciation keys

Adjust the depreciation key or keys as needed to reflect the updates for the cutoff value keys.

6.6.7 Maintain index series

Define the index series here for the net worth tax depreciation area. This index will be used for revaluation of the value upwards or downwards, based on the calculation with the index.

6.6.8 Define screen layout

Adjust the screen layout for the relevant areas with net worth tax.

6.6.9 Modify asset classes

Adjust the asset classes for net worth tax and input the default values that will populate in the master records.

6.6.10 Make chart-of-depreciation-specific entries in asset classes

Lastly, make any adjustments for chart-of-depreciation-specific entries in the asset class.

6.7 Preparations for consolidation

Depending on where a company performs consolidations, the settings in these configuration nodes may need updating. Each asset transaction type must be assigned a consolidation transaction type. Also, some transactions will require proportional values, such as retirements. Thirdly, you need to identify which depreciation areas are group depreciation areas.

6.7.1 Specify consolidation transaction types for APC transactions

Here, you assign the consolidation transaction type to match the corresponding asset transaction type, as shown in Figure 6.25.

Trans. Type	Transaction Type Name	Cons TType
000	Formal transctn type for migration (000,398,399)	
020	Acquisition:Cost-accounting area only	120
030	Acquisition in group area only	120
100	External asset acquisition	120
101	Acquisition for a negative asset	120
103	Incidental costs, non-deduct. input tax (fol.yrs)	100
105	Credit memo in invoice year	120
106	Credit memo in invoice year to affiliated company	125

Figure 6.25: Assign consolidation transaction types

6.7.2 Specify transaction types for proportional value adjustments

Some transaction types will require proportional values, so determine and define them here, as shown in Figure 6.26.

Dialog Structure

∨⌐ Transaction type
   ⌐ Value adjustment procedure

Tra	Transaction Type Name
✓ 200	Retirement without revenue
☐ 201	Retirement due to catastrophe, without revenue
☐ 206	Retirement without revenue - Finnland EVL

Figure 6.26: Proportional value adjustment transaction types

Figure 6.27 shows the consolidation transaction type that is selected for adjustments to accumulated depreciation.

Dialog Structure

∨⌐ Transaction type
   ⌐ Value adjustment procedure

Trans. Type: **200**   Retirement without revenue

Transact.	Type of adjustment to accumulated depr.	TrType
1	Ordinary depreciation	290
2	Special depreciation	290
3	Unplanned depreciation	290
4	Transfer of reserves	290
5	Investment support	290
6	Reval. acquisition value;	290
7	Reval. of depreciation	290

Figure 6.27: Assign proportional transaction types

6.7.3   Specify group depreciation areas

Identify which depreciation areas are going to be posting group values and check the GROSSTRNSF box, as shown in Figure 6.28.

Chart of dep.: 1710   Chart of Depreciation 1710 US

Ar.	Name of Depreciation Area	GrossTrnsf
01	Book Depreciation	☑
02	Book Depreciation	☑
30	Local GAAP-local currency	☐
32	IFRS in local currency	☑
33	IFRS in group currency	☑
34	Local GAAP-Group currency	☑
90	Federal Tax ACRS/MACRS	☐
91	Alternative Minimum Tax	☐
92	Adjusted Current Earnings	☐
93	Corporate Earnings & Profits	☐
94	Special Valuations	☐

Figure 6.28: Determine gross value for area

6.8 Leasing processing

With all the recent legal and statutory changes regarding leasing and lease accounting rules for US GAAP and IFRS, most companies are choosing to go with third-party software to handle the new leasing regulations. SAP is also developing a new standard solution. It might be possible that the new rules do not apply to your business and you need to set up leasing in SAP. If so, then you can define leasing types, sort versions for reporting and screen layouts, and even modify the necessary asset classes. One thing to note, except for the node to define leasing types, other configuration nodes can be reached via other configuration sections and nodes.

6.8.1 Define leasing types

Define your lease types, as shown in Figure 6.29.

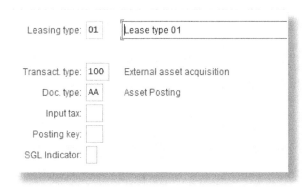

Figure 6.29: Define lease types

6.8.2   Define sort versions for leasing reports

If necessary, create a new sort version for lease type reporting, as shown in Figure 6.30.

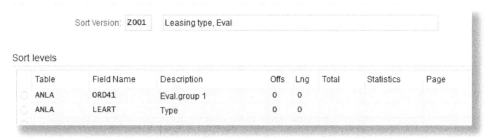

Figure 6.30: Define lease types sort version

6.8.3   Define screen layout

In this section, determine which fields are needed, and if they are required, optional, hidden, or displayed. Also, will they be maintained at the class level, asset, asset sub-number, or are they copied.

6.8.4 Modify asset classes

Not all asset classes will be needed for leases or have the right configuration for leases. If you have an asset class for leases, you can update vendor, lease type, duration in years, number of payments, and number of periods, as shown in Figure 6.31.

Class	Asset Class Description	Leas.comp.	Ty...	Yr.	Cycle	Number	Periods
5000	Low-value Assets						
6000	Leases	USSU01	01	3	1	36	36

Figure 6.31: Modify asset class for leasing

7 Master data

This chapter covers one of the great aspects about using SAP Asset Accounting—the integration with other SAP modules. With SAP Asset Accounting, you can have integration with equipment master records, internal orders, and WBS elements. Most of the time, the different phases or statuses of these objects will determine the status and out-come of the asset accounting asset master record.

At the end of the working usefulness of a WBS element, you close the WBS and the asset under construction (AUC) is retired or disposed. This is all done automatically, via configuration in the IMG.

7.1   Screen layout

Additionally, you can control the field layout for an asset under construction so that a user cannot enter a useful life for it, and therefore will not have a life to amortize or depreciate over time. You can set up different screen lay-outs for different types of assets so they can be used in different ways. The different types of layouts can be seen in Figure 7.1.

	Layou	Name of screen layout rule
☐	Y100	Real estate
☐	Y110	Buildings
☐	Y200	General machines
☐	Y300	Fixtures and fittings
☐	Y310	Vehicles
☐	Y311	Vehicles US
☐	Y320	Computers (Hardware/Software)
☐	Y330	Low value assets
☐	Y400	Assets under construction
☐	Y401	Capital investment measure

Figure 7.1: Screen layout list

7.1.1   Define screen layout for asset master data

Define the screen layout to use for the asset master records. Each logical field group contains field groupings. Adjust as needed, or use the standard options. Field groups are listed in Figure 7.2.

Figure 7.2: Define the screen layout

7.1.2   Define screen layout for asset depreciation areas

In addition to creating the layouts for asset classes, you can also create unique layouts for the depreciation areas. For example, with Tax Depreciation areas, you can create screen layouts that will include the normal items like DEPRECIATION KEY, USEFUL LIFE, depreciation start date, and depreciation calculation start date. But what you may not want to include is SCRAP VALUE, SCRAP VALUE %, INDEX SERIES, and variable depreciation portion. If these fields are not relevant to the asset depreciation area, then sometimes it is easier for the end user to not see these fields at all. A sample depreciation area layout, with the ADDITIONAL SPECIFICATIONS grouping, is shown in Figure 7.3.

Asset: 200000   0   ELEVATOR

Class: 2000   Machinery Equipment   Company Code: 1010

Area   01   Book Deprctn: Book Depreciation

Interval from 01.01.1900 to 31.12.9999

General Specifications

Depreciation Key: **LINS**   Str.-line over rem.life pro rata to zero

Useful Life: 8 /   0   Start of Calculation

Changeover year: / 0   DeprCalcStartDate:

Additional Specifications

Index series:

Variable dep.portion: 0,0000

Scrap value: 0,00   EUR

Scrap Value %: 0,00000000000

☐ Neg. Vals Allowed

🔄 More Intervals

Figure 7.3: Define the screen layout for depreciation areas

7.1.3   Specify tab layout for asset master record

The asset tabs on the asset master record can also be configured in this section of the IMG. First, define the tabs and then the field groups for each tab. This is done for the asset master records by way of the asset class, and then the tab layout is assigned to the asset classes and charts of depreciation. Figure 7.4 shows the tab pages for LAYOUT SAP1.

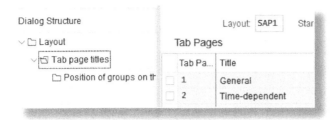

Figure 7.4: Specify the tab layout

7.1.4   Process selection criteria

In the process selection criteria section, you define the selection criterion for selecting assets via Internet or intranet transactions.

7.1.5   Activate country-specific data

When necessary, enter and set up country-specific data according to specific business needs.

7.2   User fields

SAP provides lots of flexibility in the area of custom fields that can be added to each asset master record for segmentation and reporting needs. There are four evaluation groups that can be used, and depending on the asset class layout, can be used across all asset classes, or can be limited to just specific asset classes. These user fields are variable in length, with four different user fields available with four characters, and one user field available with eight characters. These fields are prepopulated in the configuration node, and then can be selected via a drop down box in the asset master record. The user field descriptions can be changed, to be focused on the usage, and easier to understand for the end user. These user fields are not always available in every asset report, but with the use of sort variants, the user fields can be added to any asset report that utilizes a sort variant. Please see Section 9.1 Define sort versions for asset reports, to find out more. Figure 7.5 shows two items that are available in evaluation groups 0001 and 0002.

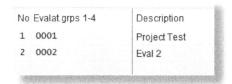

No	Evalat.grps 1-4	Description
1	0001	Project Test
2	0002	Eval 2

Figure 7.5: Specify the evaluation group values

Other user fields that work similarly include the reason for investment field, which is self-explanatory, and the environment protection indicator. Also, the asset super number is a way to group assets for reporting and categorize assets in multiple ways as needed by the business team and end users.

One more important point on user fields is that they can be defaulted in with values based on asset class. So, the user fields can be dynamic in the asset master records and updated after they are created, or they can be static and defaulted in at the time of the asset master record creation, via the asset class.

7.3   Automatic creation of equipment master records

This section provides the ability to configure the setup of asset master records so they are linked up with the equipment master records in plant maintenance. There are a few steps in the process to linking the equipment master, such as assigning the equipment category to an asset class to allow the equipment master to be created at the time the asset master is saved. The reverse is also true; you can set up unique combinations of asset class and equipment type, so that asset master records are automatically created at the time an equipment master is saved.

7.4   Specify time-independent management of organizational units

Time-independent management of organizational objects means turning off the ability to manage assets being assigned to cost centers with time intervals. Other organizational objects that can be time independent are business areas, and profit centers—indirectly through the assignment of cost centers. It is also important to note here that time-independent objects are not allowed when segment reporting is activated for the company code.

7.5 Specify cost center check across company codes

This section will provide the ability to check for cost center usage across company codes. Typically, a cost center is assigned to an asset, and that asset will live in a single company code. If this is set to active, the asset can be assigned to a cost center in another company code.

Attention: Cost center check across company codes
I would strongly suggest avoiding this setting. If you really need to assign an asset to a cost center in another company code, transfer the asset. Or, allocate the depreciation.

There is another reason for this setting; it allows for the configuration of cost centers so that they can be reassigned to a different company code. Search for SAP OSS notes for more on this setting.

7.6 Define asset search help

If the standard search help is not sufficient, use the define asset search help section for additional help.

7.7 Specify retention periods for archiving

This section provides the ability for customization of the archiving settings for asset master records and associated transactional data. Archiving is a very important aspect of system maintenance, and beyond the scope of this book, so search archiving references for more information on the how, why, when, etc.

7.8 Define validation

In the validation section, you can create the validations for fields that will help prevent inaccurate or unwanted data. Validation rules are created and then assigned to company codes. They can be run in the foreground, in the background, or both. The use of validations enables checking or validating the asset master data at the time of entry or change, which improves data accuracy in many ways. One example of a validation rule would be to check for specific cost centers entered in a specific asset class, and if the condition is not met, then present an error message to the user, and not allow the entry.

One example of a validation step would be to create a prerequisite based on company code and asset class. The check would be for a value in the field in the asset master record, or a value in the Eval Group 1 field. If the prerequisite is met and the value is not in the field, then an error message is displayed and the user will not be able to proceed until the value field is corrected to be the predetermined validation value. Validations are a very flexible tool in SAP Asset Accounting and can literally have endless possibilities for validation of the asset master data and depreciation areas. See Figure 7.6 for an example of a validation rule and step for use in SAP Asset Accounting.

Figure 7.6: Define validations

The validation setup can utilize a rule that is created by company code, field group tab, and logical field group. Then the rule can be activated or remain inactive, based on need, or any other factors.

7.9   Define substitution

Substitution settings can be designed so that when an asset master record is created, certain fields can be automatically populated with data derived from other asset characteristics. In much the same way validation steps and rules are set up, substitution steps and rules are created and then assigned to company codes. They can also be run in the foreground, in the background, or both. The key difference here is that substitutions will populate the asset master record with data derived from the asset master, and not simply validate the values of the asset master record. See Figure 7.7 for an example of a substitution rule and step that will populate a useful life of 003 when the prerequisite is met.

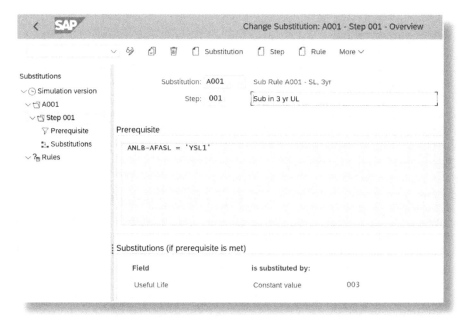

Figure 7.7: Define substitutions

7.10   Define long-term templates

Definition of a long-term template can be useful for creating a template and assigning it to an asset. There are several long-term template options available for use that can be assigned to asset classes.

7.11 Enter chart-of-depreciation-dependent user fields in asset class

This is very helpful functionality when implementing the user fields across asset classes and different charts of depreciation. Using this functionality, an asset class that is used for land can have different layouts across different charts of depreciation. For example, the asset class 1000 Land in the US chart of depreciation could have an extra field in the screen layout that is different from the asset class 1000 Land in a Canadian chart of depreciation. So, it's dependent on the needs of the business and the different reporting requirements in different countries.

7.12 Develop an enhancement for automatic assignment of inventory number

Enhancements can be done to help with automatic assignment of the inventory number. Please reference SAP Help and the Performance Assistant for more information on how this can be done via custom enhancements.

7.13 Country-specific functions

Country-specific functions are typically only needed for statutory reasons and needs. Contact a local, in-country consultant for more information and configuration.

8 Transactions

Asset transaction types help you group transactions together for use in reporting. In this chapter, you will find out about all the types of transactions, how they are grouped, and a rule of thumb on how to identify the different kind of transaction types by numerical value.

In this section, you will cover the transactions in SAP Asset Accounting that can be organized into three main groups:

► Acquisitions and Subsequent Acquisitions

► Retirements and Disposals

► Transfers

Also, SAP used logic when creating the transaction type ranges and did so by making acquisition transactions in the 100s, retirements and disposals in the 200s, and transfers in the range of 300s. By doing this, there are several advantages. One advantage of these specified ranges is in the asset history sheet and report generation. Additionally, there are other types of transactions, such as depreciation in the 600s, post-capitalization in the 400s, write-ups in the 700s, and revaluation in the 800s. Figure 8.1 shows a filtered list of the first transaction type of each the different transaction codes.

Transact. type	Transaction Type Name
✓ 100	External asset acquisition
✓ 200	Retirement without revenue
✓ 300	Retirmt transfer of prior-yr acquis. frm cap.asset
✓ 400	Post-capitalization
✓ 500	Post depreciation
✓ 600	Manual ordinary depreciation on prior-yr acquis.
✓ 700	Write-up ordinary and special depreciation
✓ 800	Post revaluation gross
✓ 900	Takeover open items APC (AuC)

Figure 8.1: Filtered transaction list

Something to keep in mind and remember from previous versions of SAP, if you wanted the transaction posting limited to specific depreciation areas, you were required to configure and limit the transaction type to only post to specific areas during posting. With SAP S/4HANA, you don't need to update or configure the transaction types in this way. At the time of posting, you can make the decision to post to specific ledgers or areas. Also, several transaction types are 'grandfathered' in to the system, in case of historical postings, but are not allowed for use anymore in the new SAP S/4HANA.

8.1 Acquisitions

Acquisition postings are the life-giving force for assets, and these transactions are the precursor for all other asset transactions. Typically, an asset is acquired with transaction type 100, and then other transactions will follow.

8.1.1 Define transaction types for acquisitions

This section shows the standard transactions for acquisitions. If necessary, you can create new ones for additional types of acquisitions, for special cases. For most companies, the standard transactions are fine. Figure 8.2 shows the EXTERNAL ASSET ACQUISITION transaction type selected.

	Transact. type	Transaction Type Name
☐	020	Acquisition:Cost-accounting area only
☐	030	Acquisition in group area only
☑	100	External asset acquisition
☐	101	Acquisition for a negative asset

Figure 8.2: Define transaction types

Inside the transaction type, there is a transaction type group used for calculation determinations. There is also the DEBIT TRANSACTION, CREDIT TRANSACTION, and CAPITALIZE FIXED ASSET options. Document type can also be seen, and defaults at the time of posting. Posting type is shown as gross or net, and whether the posting is to an affiliate or not. In the OTHER FEATURES section, the CONSOLIDATION TRANSACTION TYPE assignment and the asset history sheet group are assigned for reporting. Please see Figure 8.3 to review the internal settings for a transaction type 100, EXTERNAL ASSET ACQUISITION.

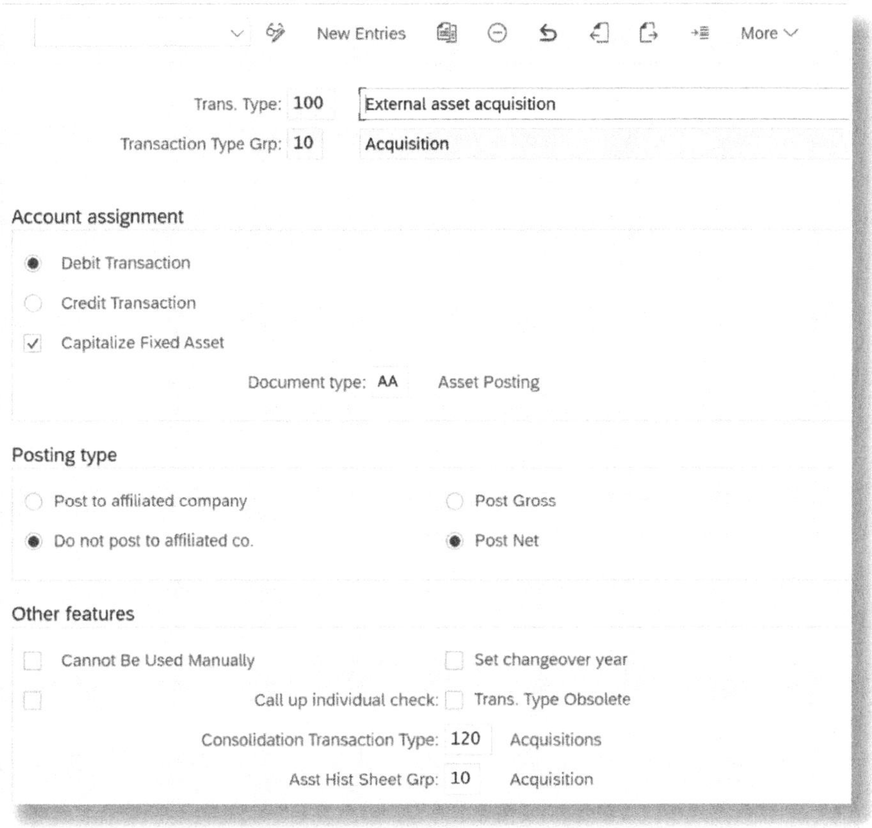

Figure 8.3: Inside the transaction type

8.1.2 Define account assignment category for asset purchase orders

In this section, you will set up account assignment categories for asset purchases via the materials management purchasing module with purchase orders, as shown in Figure 8.4.

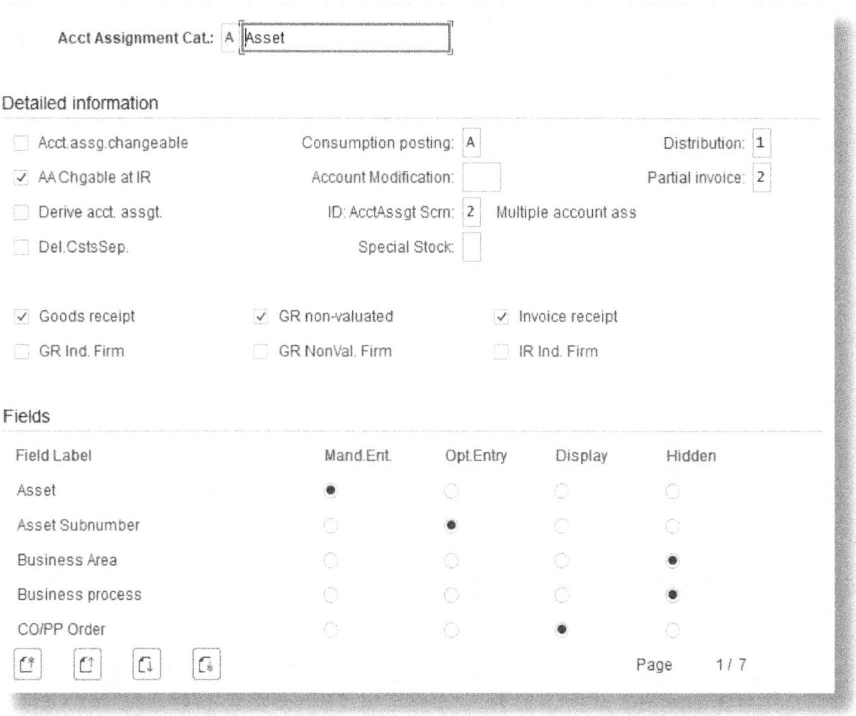

Figure 8.4: Account assignment category for asset

8.1.3   Specify asset class for creating asset from purchase order

In this section, you can identify the asset class for specific material groups, for purchased assets coming in via purchase orders, as shown in Figure 8.5.

Mat. Grp	Mat. Grp Descr.	Class	Short Text
42321700	Hip Joint Implants		
43000000	IT Broadcast Telcom		
43212100	Computer Printers	3200	Computer Hardware
43222600	Network ServiceEquip		
44000000	Office Equipment and	3000	Fixtures Fittings

Figure 8.5: Assign asset class to material group

8.1.4   Assign accounts

Similar to earlier sections, you can assign the accounts here for acquisitions, in the account determination, for the depreciation areas that post to the chart of accounts.

8.1.5   Technical clearing account for integrated asset acquisition

You can identify the clearing account for integrated asset acquisition by chart of accounts. This section is a duplicate from the earlier configuration node found in Section 3.2 Technical clearing account for integrated acquisitions.

If you need to post to a different technical clearing account based on account determination, then you need to identify the account here, with a different field control variant in the master data for the balance sheet account.

8.1.6   Allow down payment transaction types in asset classes

In this section, you identify which asset classes will allow for down payments. Two examples of these asset classes are *assets under construction*, and *assets under construction as investment measures*. As a reminder, investment measures can be internal orders or WBS elements. When set up as statistical, they are not settled at month end, when non-statistical, they do need to be settled at month end.

8.1.7   Prevent subsequent capitalization of discounts

In this section, you identify the company code that will prevent subsequent capitalization of discounts.

8.1.8   Define validation

If necessary, you can add validation rules and steps to help with the accuracy of our acquisitions. First, you create a validation and then add 'steps' to the validation. After the validation is created, you can then assign it to a transaction type group (TTG) and activate the validation. Please see Figure 8.6 for an example of how to activate or inactivate the validation.

"Validation of Posting (Asset Accounting)"

TTG	Name for the Transaction Type Group	Validation	Validation Description	Capit	
00	Annual Carryforward			Inactive	∨
10	Acquisition	AV001	Asset Acquisitions	Active	∨
11	Aquis. negative asset / CO settlement			Inactive	∨
12	Reverse acquisition in following years			Inactive	∨

Figure 8.6: Assign validation to transaction type group

8.2   Retirements

Asset retirements usually signal the end of the asset's useful life. Typically, this is done with transaction type 200, which will also deactivate the asset master record. When the retirement happens, the deactivation date on the asset master is populated with the retirement date. The asset will fall off the asset balance reports. The one report the asset does not disappear from, will be the asset retirement report.

8.2.1   Define transaction types for retirements

In this section, you will determine the transaction types for retirement. Several are standard. Please see Figure 8.7 for the start of the retirement transaction types with a prefix of '2'.

Transact. type	Transaction Type Name
200	Retirement without revenue
201	Retirement due to catastrophe, without revenue
206	Retirement without revenue - Finnland EVL
209	Retmt. of prior-yr acq. from inv.meas. w/o revenue
20A	Retirement without revenue

Figure 8.7: Define transaction types for retirement

8.2.2   Gain or loss posting

In the next several configuration nodes, you will identify the treatment for asset retirements and the gain or loss posting that will result when assets are not fully depreciated.

Determine posting variants

If a different gain or loss treatment is needed for depreciation areas, then be sure to identify the type of treatment, and assign the variant for each area. Figure 8.8 shows how Area 01 can be configured for retirements.

Figure 8.8: Define posting variant for retirement

Define transaction types for write-up due to gain/loss

This section is updated only if not all retirement gains or losses are posted to a Profit or Loss account. If updating, then review the standard transaction types and copy or modify as needed.

Determine asset for gain/loss posting per class

Here, you will identify the need to post gains or losses to a single asset within an asset class, as shown in Figure 8.9.

Class	Asset Class Description	Asset No.	SNo.
1000	Real Estate (Land)	100001	
1100	Buildings		
1200	Land Improvements		

Figure 8.9: Define for gain/loss posting

Determine asset for gain/loss individually (substitution)

If you are not posting our gain or loss to Profit or Loss accounts, then you can identify and configure substitution rules for handling the updates and postings. You can assign the revenue distribution method, as shown in Figure 8.10.

Revenue Distribution Method in Company Code

CoCd	Company Name	Rev.Dist.
1013	Fair Trade Coffee SARL	By Net Book Value
1020	Green Bike GmbH	By Net Book Value
1110	Fish and Chips Company	By Net Book Value

Figure 8.10: Define revenue distribution for retirement

Define revenue distribution for fixed asset retirement

In this section, you are going to determine how revenue is distributed for retirements, by acquisition, production costs, or by net book value.

Post net book value instead of gain/loss

In some countries, there is a legal requirement to post net book value instead of a gain or loss for the retirement. In such cases where there is a statutory requirement, enter the configuration here. This is not a standard setting, so configuration will be needed to adhere to such requirements. First, specify the company codes for net book value postings, then specify the depreciation areas for net book value posting.

8.2.3   Define validation and assign accounts

This section is similar to the asset acquisitions section, where you can define a validation, and also assign accounts for retirement.

8.3   Transfer postings

Transfer postings can be a transfer within the same company code or from one company code to another company code.

8.3.1   Define transaction types for transfers

In the case of transfers, there will be a retirement on the sending asset and then an acquisition on the receiving asset. Try to use the standard transaction types delivered by SAP. In special cases, modify where necessary.

8.3.2   Specify posting variant for retirement transfers

In some cases, there are statutory reasons for transferring the acquisition and production cost (APC) only, and not transferring the proportional value adjustments of the asset for the transfer. In these special cases, identify the transaction types for use, and then also identify the depreciation areas that need to use this APC only setting. Figure 8.11 shows the areas are not selected for APC only.

Dialog Structure		
˅ ☐ Transaction type selection	Chart of dep.: **1710** Chart of Depreciation 1710 US	
☐ Special handling of transfe	Trans. Type: **300** Retirmt transfer of prior-yr acquis. frm cap.asset	

Ar.	Name of Depreciation Area	Trans. APC only
☐ 1	Book Depreciation	☐
☐ 2	Book Depreciation	
☐ 30	Local GAAP-local currency	☐
☐ 32	IFRS in local currency	☐

Figure 8.11: Define special handling for retirement

115

8.3.3 Define validation

Define validations for transfers as needed here. Remember, these can be very powerful and incredibly useful tools for keeping accurate asset master record data.

8.4 Intercompany asset transfers

Cross-company asset transfers, or intercompany transfers, are a special type of transfer that results in a transfer of the asset master record data and values from one company code to another company code in SAP. Configuration settings around this type of transaction allow for creating different transfer variants which will determine what master data is copied over to the new asset master record, what balances are copied over, and to which areas balances are copied to in the asset in the receiving company code. For the most part, you will need to decide if you want to transfer the gross values and include the cost and accumulated depreciation, or net values, where you just send over the net book value. This can also be dependent on depreciation area and type of ledger, so be cautious and know what values are needed for each of the areas before using this transaction.

Define cross-system depreciation areas

Define the *cross-system areas* in each chart of depreciation, and then be sure to assign all areas to a cross-system area, as shown in Figure 8.12.

Cr...	Short description	Name
1	US GAAP	US GAAP
15	Local GAAP	Local GAAP
31	US GAAP	US GAAP
32	Group USD	Group USD
33	Tax Book	Tax Book Local

Figure 8.12: Define cross-system areas

Next, assign the local areas to the cross-system areas. It is important to note that these areas will be used in the transfer of the asset in the current system. Be sure to identify which areas are to be transferred and assign the correct cross-system area, as shown in Figure 8.13.

Chart of dep.: **1710**　　Chart of Depreciation 1710 US

Ar.	Dep. Area	Crs-Sys.Ar	Short description	ValAd	IdAPC
1	Book Deprctn	1	US GAAP	0	
2	Book Deprctn			1	
30	GAAP-local c	15	Local GAAP	1	
32	IFRS loc cur			0	
33	IFRS grp cur			32	
34	GAAP-Grp cur	32	Group USD	1	
90	ACRS/MACRS	33	Tax Book	1	
91	ALT MIN			90	
92	ACE			90	
93	E&P			90	
94	SV			90	

Figure 8.13: Assign local areas to cross-system areas

Define transfer variants

The list of *transfer variants* provided should be enough, but you may want to copy and create your own. Be sure you set up each variant with the correct transaction types at the next level. Gross transaction types should be assigned in the gross method variant. Additionally, make sure the company codes are set up with company IDs and the copy of specific fields are configured for the transfer variants. Figure 8.14 shows a list of the variants that are used for processing a transfer.

Variant	Name
1	Gross method
2	Net method
3	Revaluation method
4	Transfer within a company code
5	Investment measure settlement
6	Line item settlement from independent AuC
7	Gross variant (affiliated company)
8	Gross variant (non-affiliated company)
100	Joint Venture historical
101	Joint Venture current year

Figure 8.14: Transfer variants

117

In the gross method transfer variant, the retirement transactions, and the acquisition transaction types are assigned. Ensure the transaction types are set up for gross valuation, or in the case of a net method, ensure the transactions are set up for net valuation. Figure 8.15 shows retirement transactions and acquisition transactions are assigned in transfer variant 1 gross method.

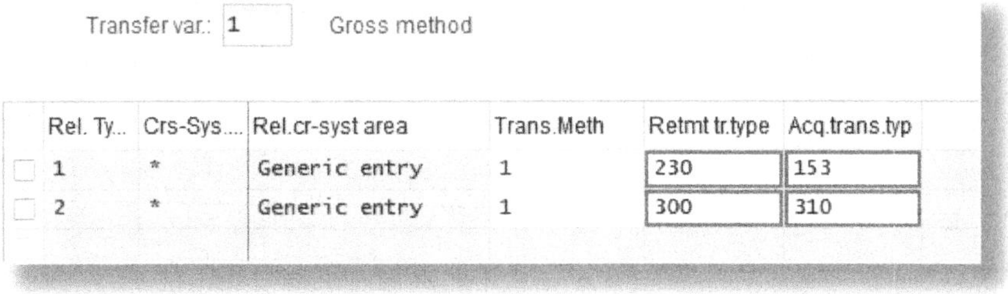

Transfer var.: 1   Gross method

Rel. Ty...	Crs-Sys....	Rel.cr-syst area	Trans.Meth	Retmt tr.type	Acq.trans.typ
1	*	Generic entry	1	230	153
2	*	Generic entry	1	300	310

Figure 8.15: Inside the gross method transfer variant

Develop enhancement for determining company code relationship

In this section, you can develop an enhancement to use in the intercompany asset transfer, and the enhancement will consider how the company code relationship is determined.

8.4.1   Specify gross or net transfer method for manual transfer

In this step, you will review and possibly reconfigure the transaction types that are used in the asset transfer process. Again, note the gross transfer variants needed to use gross transaction types. Figure 8.16 shows transaction type 153 is set up as a gross transaction type.

Trans. Type: 153   Gross interco.transf.acquis. prior-yr frm affil.co

Transaction Type Grp: 19   Acquis. of prior-yr acquis.- gross

Posting type

● Post to affiliated company   ● Post Gross

○ Do not post to affiliated co.   ○ Post Net

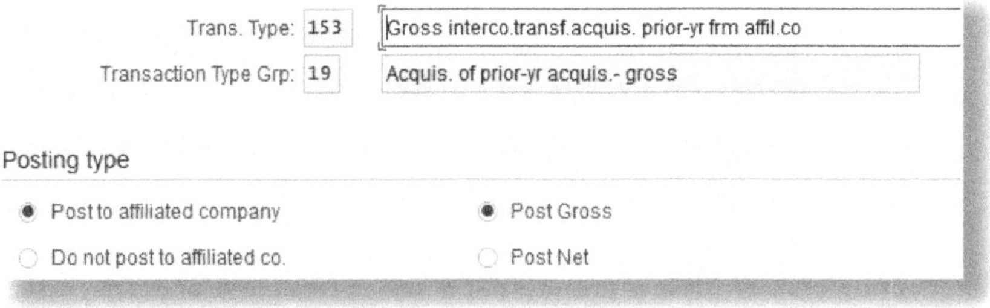

Figure 8.16: Specify gross or net posting type

118

8.4.2   Asset waybills (for South America)

Consider the configuration based on your local needs due to statutory and legal reporting. Discuss with a local consultant if assistance is needed for implementing asset waybills.

8.5   Capitalization of assets under construction

8.5.1   Define transaction types for post-capitalization

Post capitalization of assets is a special type of transaction that allows for updating the value for the asset at a later date, with respect to the asset's actual capitalization date. If the standard transactions are not sufficient, new ones can be added here.

8.6   Define transactions for manual depreciation

In this section, you can create transaction types that are designed for manual and unplanned depreciation. The easiest way to move forward with these transaction types is to use the standard transaction types, and modify the descriptions to suit the needs of the business. Something to keep in mind, in previous versions of SAP, due to certain configuration, you were forced to configure transaction types so that they only post to specific areas during posting. With SAP S/4HANA, you don't need to update or configure the transaction types in this way. At the time of posting, you can make the decision to post to specific ledgers or areas, via selection boxes and ledgers.

One example of changing a standard transaction type would revolve around US tax depreciation postings. In the case of tax depreciation postings, a transaction type can be limited to posting to the tax depreciation Area 10 in the US chart of depreciation. To do this, you would need to ensure you select the correct areas for posting. Depending on the setup for Area 10, a financial document may or may not be created. If the area is statistical, no financial document will be created. The US tax depreciation areas are normally set up as statistical areas only, and do not have financial document postings.

Also, the standard unplanned depreciation transaction type can be modified for use with local ledgers and post only in the depreciation area desired for that unplanned depreciation. For example, let's assume a US-based company has a foreign subsidiary set up in Europe. The foreign sub would have a local ledger set up for local GAAP reporting. Transaction types may be needed to post adjustments to the prior and current fiscal years' and depreciation. In this scenario, you need to ensure, at the time of posting, that you choose the correct areas to make depreciation adjustments.

If for some reason a new transaction type needs to be created, use a Y or Z in the beginning of the three-digit code to avoid the SAP reserved name spaces. Alternatively, copy the 642 and 652 transactions types, and rename them Z42 and Z52.

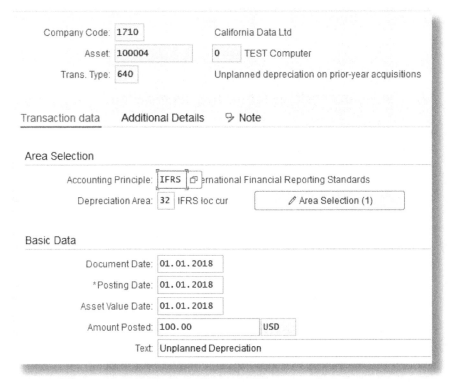

Figure 8.17: Posting to asset for specific ledger and areas

Figure 8.17 shows that Area 32 is selected for posting, and the accounting principle is IFRS. This posting, when saved, will update Area 32 and Area 33, since it is sourced with values from Area 32.

Click on the selection box next to the areas to post. Figure 8.18 shows Area 32 selected.

Select Depreciation Areas

Selected	Area	Name of Depreciation Area	AccP	Crcy
✓	32	IFRS in local currency	IFRS	USD
✓	33	IFRS in group currency	IFRS	EUR
☐	1	Book Depreciation	LG	USD
	2	Book Depreciation	LG	EUR
☐	30	Local GAAP-local currency	LG	USD
	34	Local GAAP-Group currency	LG	EUR
☐	90	Federal Tax ACRS/MACRS	LG	USD
	91	Alternative Minimum Tax	LG	USD
	92	Adjusted Current Earnings	LG	USD
	93	Corporate Earnings & Profits	LG	USD

Figure 8.18: Selecting the specific depreciation areas

8.7 Budget monitoring with statistical orders and WBS elements

In this section, you can modify the G/L accounts needed for statistical tracking of budgets with statistical orders and WBS elements. Additionally, if the field status of the G/L account needs to change, the link to that configuration item is here, too. Be sure to work closely with the G/L team to ensure that the field status is properly configured for both the needs of Asset Accounting and General Ledger accounting. As a reminder, orders and WBS elements can also be referred to as *investment measures.*

8.8 Specify default transaction types

SAP allows you to set default transaction types for different types of postings, such as acquisitions, retirements, transfers, credit memos, etc. For example, the transaction code ABAA is used for posting unplanned depreciation, and the transaction type 640 is designated as the default transaction type. See Figure 8.19.

Default transaction types for FI-AA posting transactions

Acct. transact. ID	Description	TType	Transact. Type Text
ABAA	Unplanned depreciation	640	Unplanned depreciation on prior-year acquisitions
ABAO	Asset sale without customer	210	Retirement with revenue
ABAV	Asset retirement by scrapping	200	Retirement without revenue
ABAW	Balance sheet revaluation	800	Post revaluation gross
ABGF	Credit memo in year after invoice	160	Credit memo in following year

Figure 8.19: Specify default transaction types

8.9 Determine transaction types for internal transactions

What are internal transactions and why do you want to set these up in the configuration? These are just like the default types from the previous section. One example is when depreciation is automatically posted at period end. These transaction types are standard with SAP and should not be changed, unless there are special circumstances.

8.10 Specify how default asset value date is determined

The asset value date is required on all asset postings and is often defaulted in, based on the document date of the posting. The default way in which the asset value date is derived can be changed, and it can be changed to other date values, beside the document date, as shown in Figure 8.20.

Variant: SAP_DEFAULT		Used when no variant assigned to company code

Name of transaction	Prim.Rule	Alt.Rule
Current-value depreciation	9	4
Retirement	1	
Settlement of AuC	2	
Down payment	2	
Settlement of order	2	
Revaluation	14	6
Acquisition posting for settlement of AuC	2	
Credit memo related to invoice	12	2
Investment support	9	4

Figure 8.20: Specify how asset value date is defaulted

The following list shows the collection of primary rules and alternate rules that can be used to determine how the asset value date is determined.

- ► 01 To be entered manually
- ► 02 Posting date
- ► 03 Document date
- ► 04 Earlier of either document or posting date
- ► 05 First day of period
- ► 06 First day of fiscal year
- ► 07 User-specif. fixed date
- ► 08 Current date
- ► 09 Capitalization date
- ► 10 Date of last retirement
- ► 11 First day after last retirement
- ► 12 Posting date, goods receipt
- ► 14 Date of revaluation measure

8.11 Enhancements

Enhancements can be created in the system to help with extraordinary circumstances. These types of scenarios are rare, but SAP allows the flexibility to add them. Program enhancements can be updated for line items, postings, revenue distribution in mass retirement, repayment amounts, asset value date, and mass impairments.

8.12 Maintain message types

Standard message types are here for the programs to alert the user to any errors with the potential asset update or transaction. In some scenarios, you may want to change these message types in how they are displayed to the user, either as Informational, a Warning, or as a Hard Error.

9 Information systems

This chapter covers reporting needs for SAP Asset Accounting. There are many SAP standard reports and many ways to customize the reports. Please review this chapter with consideration for how to meet specific company reporting needs for Asset Accounting.

9.1 Define sort versions for asset reports

Many of the asset balance reports do not have the entire list of asset fields that are found on an asset master record, but this deficiency can be remedied very easily by creating a special *sort version* to suit specific needs. When creating a new sort version, essentially up to five new asset fields can be added to any asset report. See Figure 9.1 for a preview of the sort versions available via the SAP standard version.

Sort Versions for Asset Reporting

Sort Vers.	Explanation
0001	Co. code/bus. area/bal. item/B/S account/class
0002	Co code/ plant / cost center
0003	Co. code / B/S acccount / asset class
0004	Co. code / property classif. /asset class
0005	Co. code / insurance type / ins. company

Figure 9.1: Sort versions for asset reporting

Drilling down into sort version 0002, shows the settings that make up the selection of values in the sort variant. The selection of the sort is shown in Figure 9.2.

Sort Version: 0002   Co code/ plant / cost center

t levels

Table	Field Name	Description	Offs	Lng	Total
ANLAV	BUKRS	Company Code	0	0	
ANLAV	WERKS	Plant	0	0	
ANLAV	KOSTL	Cost Center	0	0	

Figure 9.2: Sort variant settings

By choosing sort variant 0024 with company code and segment, the report output shows these fields as available for subtotal, sorting, and bold type. Figure 9.3 shows the report SORT VARIANT used is 0024, from an asset report example.

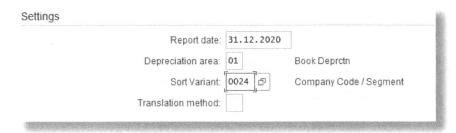

Figure 9.3: Use of sort version 0024 in an asset report

Figure 9.4 shows the SEGMENT field, which is normally not available in the standard report layout, but with the usage of the SORT VARIANT 0024, the SEGMENT field is now available.

CompanyCode   Segment

1010   1000_A

Asset	SNo.	Cap.Date	Description	Acquis.val.	Accum.dep.	Book val.	Crcy	CoCd	Segment
100003	0	31.07.2019	Computer So...	5,000.00	1,250.00-	3,750.00	EUR	1010	1000_A
100005	0	27.07.2019	Computer S1	5,000.00	2,500.00-	2,500.00	EUR	1010	1000_A
100006	0	01.01.2018	Computer Ha...	12,000.00	12,000.00-	0.00	EUR	1010	1000_A

Figure 9.4: Segment field in asset report with sort 0024

9.2   Define simulation variants for depreciation reports

This simulation tool is very useful but seldom utilized in SAP. It is helpful for making forecasts and future calculations for asset accounting master records. An example of a *simulation version* is shown in Figure 9.5.

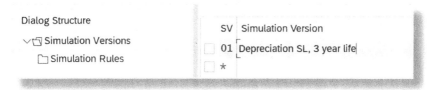

Figure 9.5: Simulation versions

In the simulation, you can temporarily replace one depreciation key with another to calculate the simulated scenario, as shown in Figure 9.6.

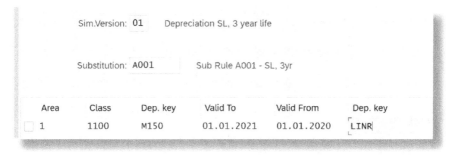

Figure 9.6: Simulation version with validity dates and key

9.3   Define SAP Queries

SAP Queries are very helpful reports and very useful for data gathering tools, for the experienced SAP user. Oftentimes, companies are reluctant to provide access to end users for fear of authoring a bad query, or having a query run all day or night and bog the system down or even crash the system. So be careful when provisioning access to queries and writing queries. If unsure, then ask for some help from an ABAP team member. Figure 9.7 shows some of the asset queries.

Query area: Global Area (Cross-client)

Query: 01		✎ Change	☐ Create
✎ QuickViewer	✎ InfoSet Query	🔍 Display	📋 Description

Queries of user group /SAPQUERY/AM: ASSET MANAGER

Nam	Title	InfoSet	Logical Database Table/View/Join	InfoSet Title
01	Inventory list	/SAPQUERY/AM01	ADA	FIAA - Inventory information
02	Real estate and similar rights	/SAPQUERY/AM02	ADA	FIAA - Real estate
03	Vehicles	/SAPQUERY/AM03	ADA	FIAA - Vehicles
04	Leasing	/SAPQUERY/AM04	ADA	FIAA - LEASING

Figure 9.7: SAP Query for asset accounting

There are many reasons to use SAP Query, and the scenarios are almost limitless. I have seen asset master data queries that will join the ANLA table, and various other tables, to pull back master data fields that just can't be obtained via the standard SAP reports.

Additionally, queries can be created that take master data and combine it with transaction data. These types of queries can be tricky because they don't always appear to work. A lot will depend on the tables chosen in the query, and how a system is configured. To name a few reasons why these queries are tricky, are the following: current year values will depend on current fiscal year, depreciation areas, intervals for cost centers, and intervals for depreciation keys and useful life. Once again, caution is the primary concern, and it is imperative to obtain accuracy, so be sure to validate the data once the query is completed. Figure 9.8 shows what it looks like to build a query.

There is always the possibility for a good debate on where queries should be created first, and then how to get those queries in production. This usually depends on where the queries are initially authored. I have always enjoyed creating the queries in a development or test system, and then in production. This particular process will depend a lot on the specific SAP system landscape and authorization levels, but I think this provides a good mix of caution and accuracy. Creating queries in development systems or test systems is harmless and allows for the perfection of the query with small amounts of data, versus the enormity of the production environment.

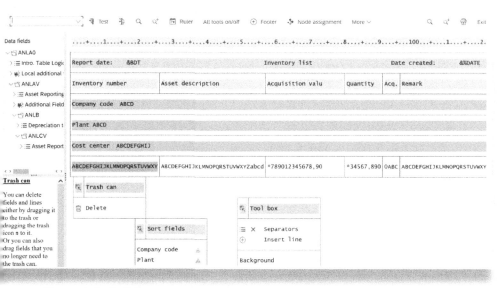

Figure 9.8: Building a query for asset accounting

9.4 Display key figures for asset accounting (SAP Fiori)

One of the cool new features of SAP S/4HANA is using the SAP Fiori tiles for shortcuts or reporting. This section allows you to display the key figures for use within SAP Asset Accounting so you can make the SAP Fiori tiles. A key figure in SAP Asset Accounting is essentially a transaction type, such as acquisitions, subsequent acquisitions, retirements, transfers, revaluation, and depreciation posted. This is very similar to how the asset history sheet is segregated into groups of transactions.

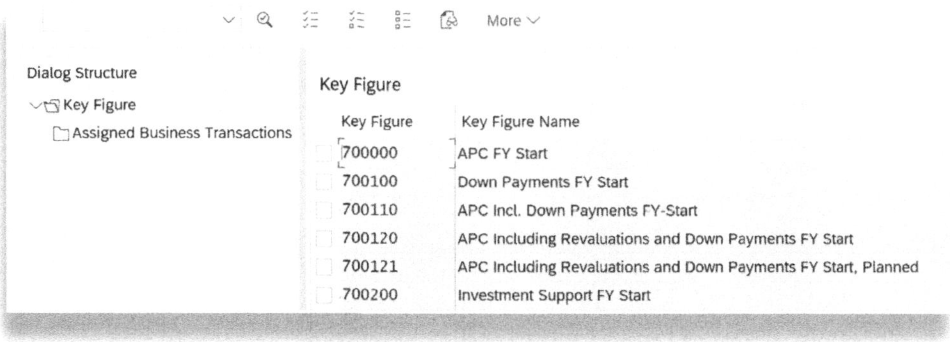

Figure 9.9: Key figures in asset accounting

Groups of transactions, or *key figures*, can be assigned to an SAP Fiori tile. This tile could be used for asset depreciation yet to be posted, retirements year to date, transfers year to date, acquisitions year to date, and so on. Note, you cannot create new key figures. Figure 9.9 shows some of the key figures available.

Key figures in SAP Asset Accounting

 Just to reiterate: you cannot create new key figures; SAP has already done this. Customizations should be, if you don't find the standards supplied sufficient, to create new groups for balances and transactions to use with SAP Fiori.

Figure 9.10 shows what subledger line item types are assigned to the key figures.

Key Figure: 700000

KF Name: APC FY Start

Assigned Business Transactions

Category	Analytical Trans. Type Category Name	Subldgr LItm Type	Subledger Line Item Type Desc.
00	Balance Carry Forward	7000	Cumulative Acquisition Costs
00	Balance Carry Forward	7002	Cumulative Investment Support
77	Legacy Data Transfer Assets under Construction APC	7000	Cumulative Acquisition Costs
97	Legacy Data Transfer AuC Investment Support	7002	Cumulative Investment Support
C7	Legacy Data Transfer FY Start	7000	Cumulative Acquisition Costs
C7	Legacy Data Transfer FY Start	7002	Cumulative Investment Support
E7	Legacy Data Transfer FY Ending Balance	7000	Cumulative Acquisition Costs
E7	Legacy Data Transfer FY Ending Balance	7002	Cumulative Investment Support

Figure 9.10: Business transactions in key figure balances

9.5 Define key figure groups for asset balances (SAP Fiori)

This section defines key figure groups for asset balances for use with SAP Fiori tiles. You can assign the analytical transaction type, or what the asset line items will be, to the KEY FIGURE GROUPS, as shown in Figure 9.11.

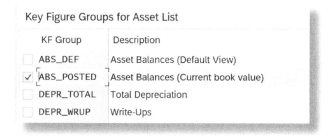

Key Figure Groups for Asset List

KF Group	Description
☐ ABS_DEF	Asset Balances (Default View)
☑ ABS_POSTED	Asset Balances (Current book value)
☐ DEPR_TOTAL	Total Depreciation
☐ DEPR_WRUP	Write-Ups

Figure 9.11: Key figure groups for asset balances

The sort sequence for the key figure groups can be changed as needed, or left alone as an SAP standard sequence. See an example in Figure 9.12.

Key Figure Group: **ABS_POSTED**

Create/Change Key Figure Groups of Asset Accounting (ABS)

Key Figure	Key Figure Name	Sequence
☐ 10700110	APC at Reporting Date	1
☐ 10700300	Revaluation APC at Reporting Date, Posted	6
☐ 10700400	Revaluation Ordinary Depreciation at Reporting Date, Posted	7
☐ 10700500	Ordinary Depreciation at Reporting Date, Posted	2
☐ 10700600	Special Depreciation at Reporting Date, Posted	3
☐ 10700700	Unplanned Depreciation at Reporting Date, Posted	4
☐ 10700800	Transfer of Reserves at Reporting Date, Posted	5
☐ 10790400	Net Book Value at Reporting Date	8
☐		

Figure 9.12: Key figure groups sequence

9.6 Define key figure groups for asset transactions (SAP Fiori)

Similar to the groups for balances, you can also set up groups for asset transactions for use with SAP Fiori. See Figure 9.13.

Key Figure Groups Asset Transactions

	KF Group	Description
✓	TRANS_ACQ	Acquisitions
☐	TRANS_ALL	All Transactions
☐	TRANS_RET	Retirements
☐	TRANS_TRN	Transfer
☐		

Figure 9.13: Key figure groups for asset transactions

KEY FIGURE GROUPS show the key figures that are assigned and this will allude to what values and line items you should see in the corresponding report output. A list of the key figures can be seen in Figure 9.14.

Key Figure Group: TRANS_ACQ

Key Figures

Key Figure	Key Figure Name
1700000	Acquisition (Gross) - APC
1700200	Acquisition (Gross) - Investment Support
1700300	Acquisition (Gross) - Revaluation APC
1700400	Acquisition (Gross) - Revaluation Ordinary Depreciation
1700500	Acquisition (Gross) - Ordinary Depreciation
1700600	Acquisition (Gross) - Special Depreciation
1700700	Acqsitn (Gross) - Unplanned Deprec.(Write-Down to Going-Concern Value)
1700800	Acquisition (Gross) - Transfer of Reserves
3710000	Intracompany Transfer of Current-Year Acquisitions - APC

Figure 9.14: Key figure for asset transactions

9.7 Asset history sheet

The *asset history sheet* is an incredible reporting tool and very powerful in the area of Asset Accounting. It is very important to understand what this tool does, and how it can be utilized for the creation of all types of asset reporting. Essentially, the asset history sheet allows for flexible report creation based on the grouping of asset transactions, so that like transactions will appear in a columnar-type report format.

A very simple asset history sheet example would be a monthly or quarterly report for reconciliation of assets. In columnar format, you could have asset acquisitions, asset retirements, and asset transfers. Then you can have another column with the difference to come up with your ending activity balance for the period. This is a relatively easy report to create, and simple to configure, but it relies upon the user base to be consistent with the usage of the transactions in the asset ledger.

For example, if you have a report such as this and are interested in the retirements section, this could cause your reports to be skewed one way or another. Typically, when an asset is disposed or retired, it is done so with a transaction type in the 200 series of transactions. If the user decides to reverse the acquisition, and not retire the asset, then the transaction will be a negative acquisition, rather than a retirement. Conversely, if you are interested in acquisitions, and the user decides to retire the asset in place of reversing the asset acquisition, then your retirements and acquisitions will be off for that period.

A consistent approach is always to reverse a transaction when a mistake has been made, such as an incorrect posting to the asset, creating the asset in the wrong asset class, etc. SAP understands mistakes will be made, and the best way to address the issue is to reverse the transaction with TRANS-ACTION CODE AB08, if it originated in the asset module; or the journal entry, if it originated elsewhere, upstream in the procurement process. If you can follow this reversal approach consistently, then you should achieve better and more accurate reporting.

There are always exceptions to the normal course of business, and some-times simply reversing is not an option. The next best option could be a mass retirement, with correcting journal entries, or some form of neutral-izing entries in the General Ledger. This is not always the cleanest way of fixing the incorrect transactions that are causing the issue, but it can be the most efficient way in a pinch, and when time is sensitive, at a period closing like month end or quarter end.

9.8   Rename value fields for asset explorer

The ability to change the names of the fields in the asset explorer is a nice feature for those who really like to customize. Please note, these value fields are not the same as the value fields in controlling and profitability analysis. Figure 9.15 shows a list of all fields in Area 01 that are available for name changes.

Chart of dep.: 1710 Chart of Depreciation 1710

Depreciat. Area: 1 Book Depreciation

No	Short name	Description
0	APC	Acquisition value
1	APC	Acquisition value
2	Inv.supprt	Investment support
3	Revaluat.	Revaluation
11	Transf.res	Transfer reserve
12	Ord. dep.	Ordinary deprec.
13	Spec.dep.	Special depreciation
14	Unplnd.dep	Unplanned dep.
20	Revaluat.	Revaluation ord.dep.
21	Write-up	Write-up
30	Interest	Interest
31	Reserves	Trsfr cum.reserves
32	Ord. dep.	Accum. ord. depr.
33	Spec.dep.	Cum.special dep.
34	Unplnd.dep	Cum.unplanned dep.
90	Net bk.val	Net book value

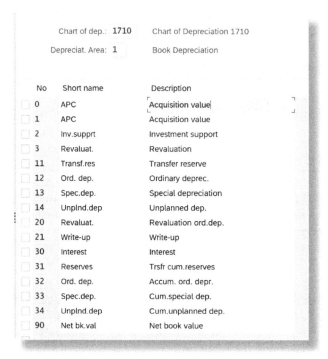

Figure 9.15: Value field names for asset accounting

9.9 Define currency translation methods

Defining *currency translation methods* for use with asset reporting may not be necessary for most, but the option to do so is here. Figure 9.16 shows an example of a translation using USD with exchange rate type M, and sourced via the acquisition date.

Translatn: 01 USD AT THE M RATE

* Currency: USD United States Dollar

* Exch. Rate Type: M Standard translation at average rate

* Transl. on: 4 Acquis. date

Day:

Month:

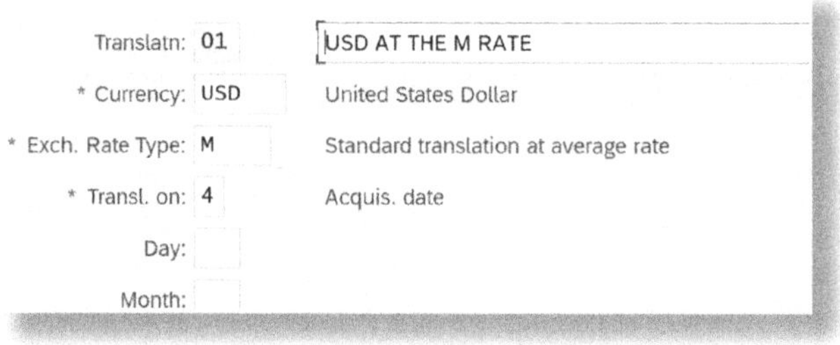

Figure 9.16: Currency translation method in asset accounting

9.10 Define or assign forms

When you have the need to define or assign forms, this is the place to do it. The forms are for printing labels or bar codes and can be customized and assigned by asset class. Most likely, you will want to copy the standard form and customize it. Customizing forms usually requires the help of an ABAP developer or a very experienced Asset Accounting consultant. Before implementation, review this functionality with different user groups and check with a local consultant for how best to use this functionality. Figure 9.17 shows where you assign the form to the asset class.

Class	Asset Class Description	Layout set name
1000	Real Estate (Land)	Z_LAND
1100	Buildings	Z_BLDG
1200	Land Improvements	
1500	Leasehold Improvements	

Figure 9.17: Assign form to asset class

9.11 Enhancements

Enhancements are a great way to improve asset accounting reporting, and can easily be done with the help from the ABAP team, and review of online SAP notes. Some of the typical enhancements for SAP Asset Accounting are currency translation methods, key descriptions for output, and the output of the asset number.

9.12 Country-specific functions

Here is where you can update country-specific settings for asset accounting reports, and due to the complexity of statutory requirements, are considered beyond the scope of this book. It is in your best interest to have a local consultant help you navigate your way through the legal and statutory requirements that can be enhanced or required in this section. Also, be sure to review the SAP OSS notes regarding the country-specific reporting.

10 Asset data transfer

This chapter covers how to transfer legacy assets into SAP. There are many settings to be aware of prior to adding legacy assets, and they are all covered in this section.

In my opinion, this is one of the more important, or next-to-most important sections, of the asset configuration. Not only does this section cover how you transfer legacy data into the asset module, but if it is not done correctly, it will cause lingering issues for years to come. If the values are not converted correctly, or the depreciation parameters are not set up correctly, then you will see issues crop up from time to time over the course of the assets' lives, until they are fixed, or fully depreciated. The latter point could take years to resolve.

Be sure to pay extremely close attention to how the configuration is set up for each depreciation area, and also be sure that the correct parameters are used in the initial setup for the legacy assets. If you have experience with previous versions of SAP, before SAP S/4HANA, you will notice quite a few changes in the legacy data transfer configuration.

10.1 Parameters for data transfer

This section defines the *transfer date* and document type to use for the legacy data transfer. But before starting on the legacy data transfer, make sure you check the last closed fiscal year in the company code for data that you are transferring. Figure 10.1 shows the last closed fiscal year as 2016, so legacy data in fiscal year 2017 will be loaded. Be sure to check all the ledgers for the company code, if there is more than one.

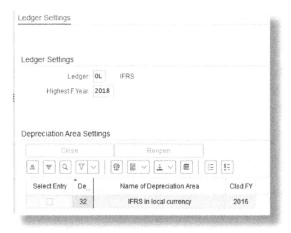

Figure 10.1: Asset data transfer IMG

10.1.1 Define transfer date and additional parameters

The transfer date is a point in time for which all legacy assets must have a capitalization date that is older than the transfer date. So, in this example, the date of last posting in the legacy system will be December 31, 2016, since the transfer date is January 1, 2017. This is shown in Figure 10.2 for the second sequence of legacy data transfers.

In the GENERAL SETTINGS tab, you can see if the COMPANY CODE is locked or productive for legacy transfers, if you are still in testing mode, or if the asset is deactivated. See Figure 10.3.

General Information

        Company Code: 1710   California Data Ltd

        Country Key: US

General Settings   Legacy Data Transfer

Current Settings for Legacy Data Transfer

        Sequence Number: 2

        Transfer Date: 01/01/2017

        Legacy Data Transfer Status: Ongoing

        Document Type: UE Data Transfer

        Comment: TEST CASE

        Suppress Depreciation Calculation:

History of Legacy Data Transfers

Seq.No.	Transfer Date	Legacy Transfer Status	Document Type	No Dep.Cal
2	01/01/2017	Ongoing	UE	
1	12/31/2015	Completed	UE	

Figure 10.2: Define legacy transfer date and sequence

General Information

        Company Code: 1710   California Data Ltd   Chart of Accounts: YCOA

        Country Key: US

General Settings   Legacy Data Transfer

General Settings for Company Code

        Company Code Status: For Testing

        Company Code Locked:

Figure 10.3: Define company code status

139

Keep in mind that the general settings are also in this section, and they help determine when the last fiscal year closed for assets. The last fiscal year closed is also tied to the ledger, and can be different depending on the ledger. For those who have used SAP in versions prior to SAP S/4HANA, you might notice that the year-end closing is not the same as it used to be, and this new method of closing by ledger is not done simply by depreciation area in a company code. Please review Figure 10.4 to see the closing method by ledger.

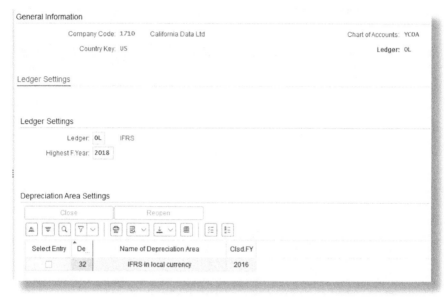

Figure 10.4: General settings for transfer

10.1.2 Specify offsetting account for legacy data transfer

The offsetting account for legacy data transfer is a balance sheet account, and it is a zero-balance account, or should be zero after the legacy transfer is completed. It will act as a temporary clearing account during the legacy data transfer process. See the account configuration in Figure 10.5.

Offsetting Account for Legacy Data Transfer

ChAc	G/L Account
L000	39913000
LF01	219099
LRE1	39913000
R100	39913000
SAFI	10360005
YCOA	39913000

Figure 10.5: Offsetting account for legacy transfer

10.1.3 Define transaction types for transfer of open items

There is a high probability that you will not need to change anything here. The transaction types provided for legacy data transfer should be sufficient, as shown in Figure 10.6. If you need to create additional items, be specific and declarative with the naming convention.

Transact. type	Transaction Type Name
900	Takeover open items APC (AuC)
910	Takeover open down payments
970	Asset Data Transfer case 1
980	Asset Data Transfer case 2
J02	Investments in State sponsored area (asset side)

Figure 10.6: Define transaction types for transfer of open items

One thing to be sure of is that if you do need to make changes here, please be sure to look at the underlying details for the transaction type, and double check for accuracy. In the example shown in Figure 10.7, be sure to note the value for the asset history sheet group to enable reporting on the legacy transfers in the history sheet.

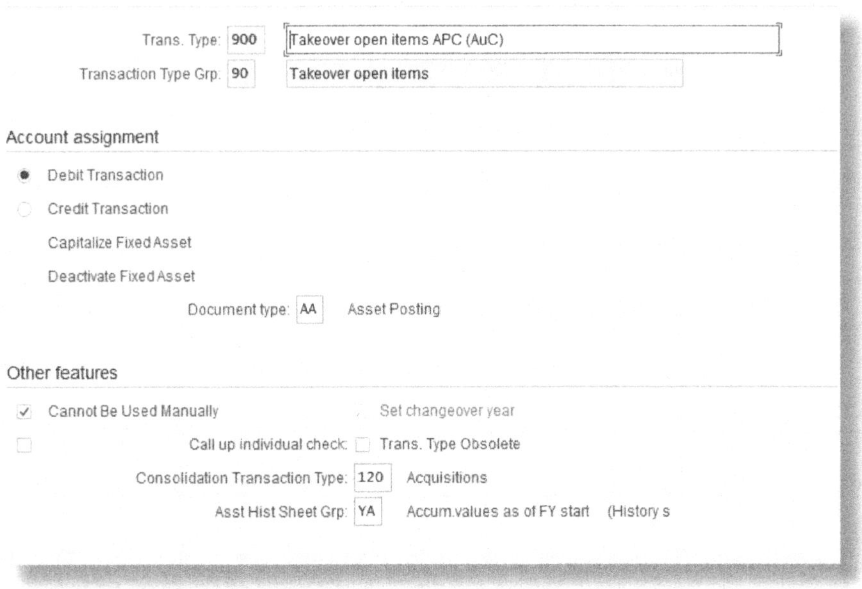

Trans. Type: 900   Takeover open items APC (AuC)

Transaction Type Grp. 90   Takeover open items

Account assignment

● Debit Transaction

○ Credit Transaction

Capitalize Fixed Asset

Deactivate Fixed Asset

Document type: AA   Asset Posting

Other features

☑ Cannot Be Used Manually   Set changeover year

☐   Call up individual check: ☐ Trans. Type Obsolete

Consolidation Transaction Type: 120   Acquisitions

Asst Hist Sheet Grp: YA   Accum.values as of FY start   (History s

Figure 10.7: Inside a transaction type for transfer of open items

10.2 Manual data transfer

10.2.1 Legacy fixed asset

This section covers the different transactions that are used to transfer legacy fixed assets.

Create master data for legacy fixed assets

When creating legacy asset data via AS91 transaction code, you first need to create the master data, and then add the legacy values. Please note, for users who have previous experience in other versions of SAP, this process has changed. After updating the values, there will be a document posted in each ledger, and the posting period variant will have to be open on the day of the legacy transfer date to allow the posting. Following are some examples.

Here is an example of the legacy asset creation, and the capitalization date is always required. This date needs to be before the transfer date, as shown in Figure 10.8.

Figure 10.8: Create legacy master data for asset

Tip regarding Legacy Assets

This section shows you how legacy assets are created in SAP. This special method of creating a legacy asset is very important to consider when adding assets as a result of when your company acquires another company, and the acquired assets need to be added to the SAP system. If you are not sure how to proceed, it is wise to seek help from your local consultant.

Change master data for legacy asset

After creating the master data updates for the legacy asset, use transaction code AS92 to change the asset values. Note, you will need to enter at least the values for cost or acquisition value, and also accumulated depreciation up to the transfer date. If you are transferring legacy data during the fiscal year, then you will also need to update year-to-date depreciation data, up to the last period posted in the legacy system. Please review all the areas and all the values closely to ensure accuracy. If you don't do this correctly the first time, you will have to reverse the financial document that gets posted. Please review Figure 10.9 to see an example of the areas and values that need to be updated for legacy transfers.

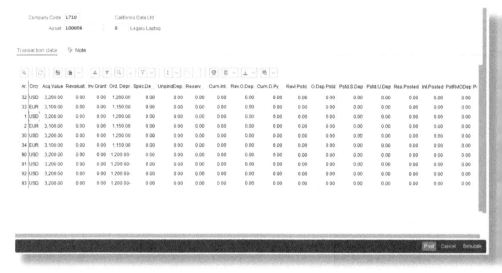

| | Company Code | 1710 | | California Data Ltd | | | | | | | | | | | | | |
| | Asset | 100006 | 0 | Legacy Laptop | | | | | | | | | | | | | |

Transaction data   🗏 Note

Ar.	Crcy	Acq.Value	Revaluat	Inv.Grant	Ord. Depr.	Spec.De	UnpIndDep.	Reserv	Cum.Int.	Rev.O.Dep.	Cum.D.Py	Revl.Pstd.	O.Dep.Pstd	Pstd.S.Dep	Pstd.U.Dep	Res.Posted	Int.Posted	PstRMODep	P...
32	USD	3,200.00	0.00	0.00	1,200.00	0.00	0.00	0.00	0.00	0.00	0.00	0.00	0.00	0.00	0.00	0.00	0.00	0.00
33	EUR	3,100.00	0.00	0.00	1,150.00	0.00	0.00	0.00	0.00	0.00	0.00	0.00	0.00	0.00	0.00	0.00	0.00	0.00
1	USD	3,200.00	0.00	0.00	1,200.00	0.00	0.00	0.00	0.00	0.00	0.00	0.00	0.00	0.00	0.00	0.00	0.00	0.00
2	EUR	3,100.00	0.00	0.00	1,150.00	0.00	0.00	0.00	0.00	0.00	0.00	0.00	0.00	0.00	0.00	0.00	0.00	0.00
30	USD	3,200.00	0.00	0.00	1,200.00	0.00	0.00	0.00	0.00	0.00	0.00	0.00	0.00	0.00	0.00	0.00	0.00	0.00
34	EUR	3,100.00	0.00	0.00	1,150.00	0.00	0.00	0.00	0.00	0.00	0.00	0.00	0.00	0.00	0.00	0.00	0.00	0.00
90	USD	3,200.00	0.00	0.00	1,200.00-	0.00	0.00	0.00	0.00	0.00	0.00	0.00	0.00	0.00	0.00	0.00	0.00	0.00
91	USD	3,200.00	0.00	0.00	1,200.00-	0.00	0.00	0.00	0.00	0.00	0.00	0.00	0.00	0.00	0.00	0.00	0.00	0.00
92	USD	3,200.00	0.00	0.00	1,200.00-	0.00	0.00	0.00	0.00	0.00	0.00	0.00	0.00	0.00	0.00	0.00	0.00	0.00
93	USD	3,200.00	0.00	0.00	1,200.00-	0.00	0.00	0.00	0.00	0.00	0.00	0.00	0.00	0.00	0.00	0.00	0.00	0.00

Post   Cancel   Simulate

Figure 10.9: Post values for legacy asset master data

After adding the values and changes to the legacy asset, click on the POST button, and look for the message update and document numbering that corresponds to each ledger, as shown in Figure 10.10.

		Document lines: Display messages		×

0	0	⚠ 0	2

Type	Item	Message Text	LTxt
■	001	Asset transaction was posted with document no. 1710 0400000001 in acctg princ. IFRS	⑦
■	002	Asset transaction was posted with document no. 1710 7000000071 in acctg princ. LG	⑦

⊘   ⑦   🔍 Technical Information   ⊡   ⊗

Figure 10.10: Post values for legacy asset master data.

If you display the asset via transaction code AS93, display legacy asset; other display, AS03; or display asset, you can drill down to the financial documents that are posted for each legacy asset. Remember from the earlier configuration step, where you updated the offsetting account for legacy data transfer, and you can see that account being used to offset the legacy data transfer in this document. Again, note, there is a financial document for each ledger, so please review the document in Figure 10.11.

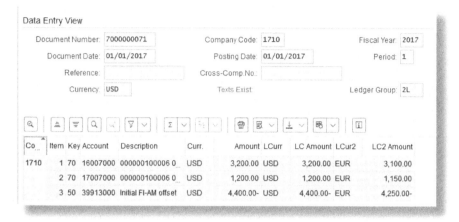

Figure 10.11: Legacy asset value posting in financial document

Display master data for legacy asset

The transaction code for this item is AS93, and can be used to display the legacy asset. Be sure to include this transaction code in all FICO display roles, so the support, functional, and business teams can all utilize this display code.

Create master data for sub-number for legacy asset

If you are using sub-numbering for assets, then be sure to utilize AS94 transaction code; other than the sub-number, it is the same as a normal legacy asset without a sub-number. But please note, certain master data will be copied with reference to the original asset number.

Post transfer values

You can reach this step via transaction code ABLDT, and it is similar to the AS92 screen shot from earlier, Figure 10.9, where you updated the values. One thing to note, if you need to update the values for the asset, be sure to reverse the earlier document that was created, before posting the new one, for the adjusted values. Note that in different areas, you need to enter different currency amounts, as shown in Figure 10.12.

145

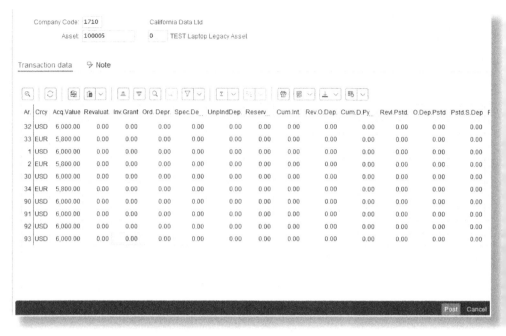

Company Code: 1710   California Data Ltd
Asset: 100005   0   TEST Laptop Legacy Asset

Transaction data   ☟ Note

Ar.	Crcy	Acq.Value	Revaluat.	Inv.Grant	Ord. Depr.	Spec.De.	UnpIndDep.	Reserv.	Cum.Int.	Rev.O.Dep.	Cum.D.Py.	Revl.Pstd.	O.Dep.Pstd	Pstd.S.Dep	F
32	USD	6,000.00	0.00	0.00	0.00	0.00	0.00	0.00	0.00	0.00	0.00	0.00	0.00	0.00	
33	EUR	5,800.00	0.00	0.00	0.00	0.00	0.00	0.00	0.00	0.00	0.00	0.00	0.00	0.00	
1	USD	6,000.00	0.00	0.00	0.00	0.00	0.00	0.00	0.00	0.00	0.00	0.00	0.00	0.00	
2	EUR	5,800.00	0.00	0.00	0.00	0.00	0.00	0.00	0.00	0.00	0.00	0.00	0.00	0.00	
30	USD	6,000.00	0.00	0.00	0.00	0.00	0.00	0.00	0.00	0.00	0.00	0.00	0.00	0.00	
34	EUR	5,800.00	0.00	0.00	0.00	0.00	0.00	0.00	0.00	0.00	0.00	0.00	0.00	0.00	
90	USD	6,000.00	0.00	0.00	0.00	0.00	0.00	0.00	0.00	0.00	0.00	0.00	0.00	0.00	
91	USD	6,000.00	0.00	0.00	0.00	0.00	0.00	0.00	0.00	0.00	0.00	0.00	0.00	0.00	
92	USD	6,000.00	0.00	0.00	0.00	0.00	0.00	0.00	0.00	0.00	0.00	0.00	0.00	0.00	
93	USD	6,000.00	0.00	0.00	0.00	0.00	0.00	0.00	0.00	0.00	0.00	0.00	0.00	0.00	

Post   Cancel

Figure 10.12: Post transfer values for legacy asset

Data transfer during the fiscal year: transfer line items

One thing that you may need to do when transferring assets during the fiscal year is update or add transactions to those legacy assets that happened during the year, before the transfer takes place. These are transactions that happened while the asset was in the legacy system. Since these transactions will impact the current year calculations, they need to be added to allow for the proper calculation of depreciation by SAP. This transaction is very similar to transaction code ABSO, in that you will need to choose an asset transaction type to post the transaction. Note that the dates will all be during the current fiscal year, and will be prior to the legacy transfer date. Note the dates in Figure 10.13.

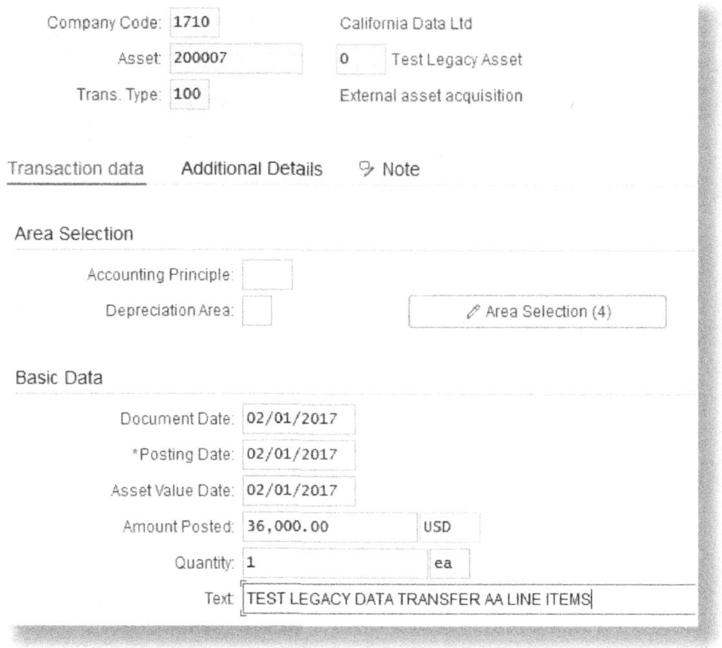

Company Code:	1710	California Data Ltd	
Asset:	200007	0	Test Legacy Asset
Trans. Type:	100	External asset acquisition	

Transaction data   Additional Details   ✑ Note

Area Selection

Accounting Principle:	
Depreciation Area:	✐ Area Selection (4)

Basic Data

Document Date:	02/01/2017	
*Posting Date:	02/01/2017	
Asset Value Date:	02/01/2017	
Amount Posted:	36,000.00	USD
Quantity:	1	ea
Text:	TEST LEGACY DATA TRANSFER AA LINE ITEMS	

Figure 10.13: Data transfer during the fiscal year

Assets under construction with line item management and transfer

This transaction is very similar to transaction code ABSO, and allows you to post line items to the asset under construction that is being transferred from the legacy system. Be sure to load the assets under construction here with any line items that you are going to want to settle to capital assets in the future, in your current SAP system. See Figure 10.14 where transaction type 985 is used to transfer open items.

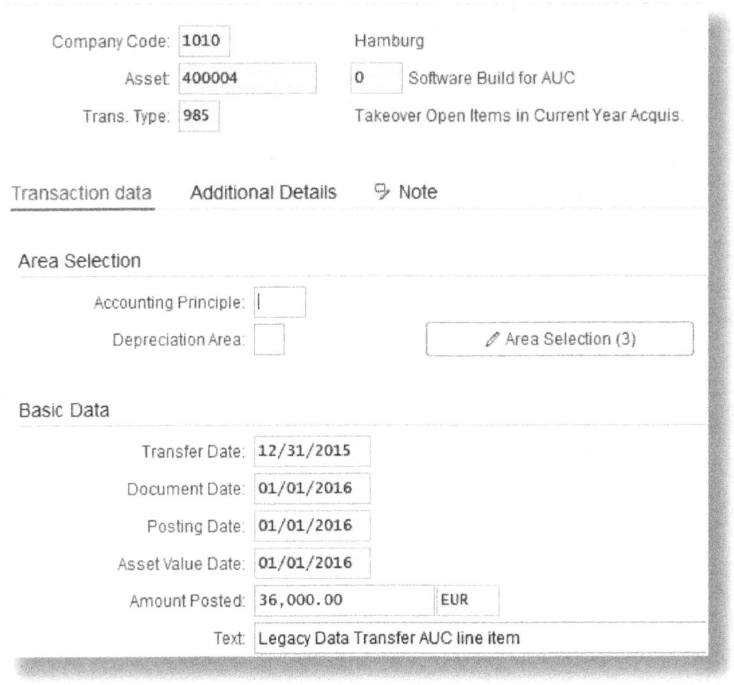

Company Code: 1010   Hamburg
Asset: 400004   0   Software Build for AUC
Trans. Type: 985   Takeover Open Items in Current Year Acquis.

Transaction data   Additional Details   ⊕ Note

Area Selection

Accounting Principle: |
Depreciation Area: ✏ Area Selection (3)

Basic Data

Transfer Date: 12/31/2015
Document Date: 01/01/2016
Posting Date: 01/01/2016
Asset Value Date: 01/01/2016
Amount Posted: 36,000.00   EUR
Text: Legacy Data Transfer AUC line item

Figure 10.14: Assets under construction legacy data transfer

10.2.2 Legacy group asset

The transfer of legacy data for group assets is very similar to the process you just walked through. Be sure to create the master data and then post the values. Documents will be posted to update the General Ledger with legacy values.

10.2.3 Legacy transfer using Microsoft Excel

You can use Microsoft Excel to load a spreadsheet and then use that sheet to upload to SAP. Follow the directions in SAP Help, and be sure to copy and paste appropriately into Excel. You will need to build the worksheet with the values before you can upload the file. Be sure to use the online help to get the correct structure of the upload sheet. The program name for this transaction code is SAPMALSMEX, and you may need some help from your ABAP team to get the fields and columns aligned in the worksheet or upload file. The transaction code for this AS100.

11 Preparations for going live

This chapter is a great way to summarize the needs for SAP Asset Accounting during the initial go-live phase of the project. From an SAP FICO support point of view, this section may require coordination with other teams, such as Security to help with authorizations and workflow tasks. But if you have gotten this far, congratulations, because you are almost ready to go live with SAP Asset Accounting.

11.1 Authorization management

Management of *authorizations* is a complex task and will require input from your Security and Authorizations team. Get started early on this and don't postpone this activity. This activity will require several iterations of review and testing, so be sure to allocate your time and resources accordingly.

If you are new to SAP and new to the concepts or roles in SAP, then it is time to study! Please review Figure 11.1; it illustrates a simple example of an asset role that provides display access. It provides three different display transactions: the asset explorer, display asset master record, and display asset document.

Figure 11.1: Preparations for going live IMG

These roles are combined together and assigned to a user ID in SAP. Once the roles are assigned to the user, the user is granted access to the transactions. For more information on roles and security, please discuss with your SAP Security team.

11.1.1 Maintain authorizations

In this section, you want to review and make sure you have the appropriate authorizations maintained. You may need to ask for help here from the ABAP team or the SAP Security team, since they will be tasked with creating and maintaining the roles and authorizations for your SAP system. Please see Figure 11.2 to see an overview for the roles and the tabs that must be maintained.

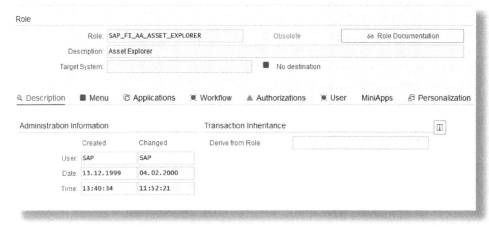

Figure 11.2: Maintain authorizations

11.1.2 Assign workflow tasks

Similar to the last section, if you are not comfortable or experienced with the workflow in SAP, it would be best to engage some help from a resident team member who is knowledgeable about SAP Workflows, or engage an SAP Workflow consultant for help. Figure 11.3 shows that workflows must be assigned agents, and the linking must be activated.

Application Component Abbre...	Application Component Description	Agent Assignment	Event Linkage
⌄ 🗂 FI-AA-AA	Basic Functions	🔗 Assign Agents	🗓 Activate event linking
📁 FI-AA-AA-MA	Asset Maintenance		
＞ 📁 FI-AA-AA-BV	Basic Valuation Functions		
＞ 📁 FI-AA-AA-FY	Fiscal Year Specifications		
＞ 📁 FI-AA-AA-DE	Depreciation		
＞ 📁 FI-AA-AA-TR	Transactions		
📁 FI-AA-AA-CL	Closing Operations		

Figure 11.3: Assign workflow tasks

11.1.3 Process asset views

The asset view is an additional step to help set up special views for different members of the organization. You will want to work with the Security and Authorization teams to ensure this is used correctly, and you have each team set up with the appropriate authorizations and views. Figure 11.4 shows the different asset views that are available in SAP.

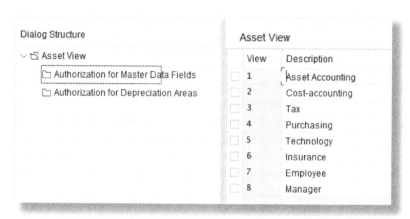

Figure 11.4: Process asset views

11.2 Check consistency

This section allows you do to do a consistency check on several areas of asset configuration. Asset classes, charts of depreciation, company codes, depreciation areas, asset general ledger accounts, and customizing can all get a consistency check, and allow you to move closer to completion of the company code and system go live. See Figure 11.5 for a list of possible consistency checks.

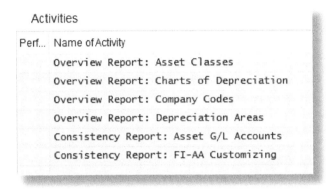

Activities

Perf...	Name of Activity
	Overview Report: Asset Classes
	Overview Report: Charts of Depreciation
	Overview Report: Company Codes
	Overview Report: Depreciation Areas
	Consistency Report: Asset G/L Accounts
	Consistency Report: FI-AA Customizing

Figure 11.5: Consistency checks

11.3 Production startup

11.3.1 Accounts approach—set/reset reconciliation accounts for parallel valuation

Depending on how you move forward in SAP S/4HANA, this configuration may not be necessary. In previous versions of SAP, one would need to change the reconciliation account setting to allow for manual postings to the asset accounts. This was normally done during the asset takeover phase, and these accounts would be turned off for reconciliation with the G/L, to load the takeover balances for acquisition and accumulated depreciation. This is not necessary if you go with the ledger approach. If you are not sure of your approach, please read through the online help, and consider the steps needed for either approach: accounts or ledger.

11.3.2 Define settings for company code

In this section, you can lock the company code from being used for testing activities. This will disable the transaction from resetting the company code data and deleting it. Once you have gone live with a company code in production, be sure to select COMPANY CODE LOCKED in the GENERAL

SETTINGS FOR COMPANY CODE section. And also set the COMPANY CODE STATUS field as PRODUCTIVE, as shown in Figure 11.6.

Figure 11.6: Set company code status to productive

11.3.3 Activate new asset accounting (new customers)

Once you are up and running in SAP S/4HANA, you need to activate the system, once per client, to engage the new functionality. After activation, the status will show as ACTIVE. Be sure to read through the documentation, as there are some limitations with settings regarding lease accounting and real estate management. See Figure 11.7 for an illustration of an active setting.

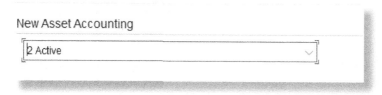

Figure 11.7: Set company code status to active

11.4 Tools

In this section you can update the company code fiscal year, and also execute closing of the fiscal year, if necessary.

11.4.1 Reset company code

Be careful here, and only use *reset company code* with great caution. This functionality is extremely powerful and can really come in handy during development and testing for preliminary go-live environments. By using this transaction code, you can delete all asset master data and asset transactional data for the company code

> **Attention: Reset company code**
>
> Please, please, please, be careful, and use sparingly. It is recommended that this is never ever used in a production environment, for obvious reasons. Please limit usage to development and test systems.

See Figure 11.8 for the warning message provided by SAP.

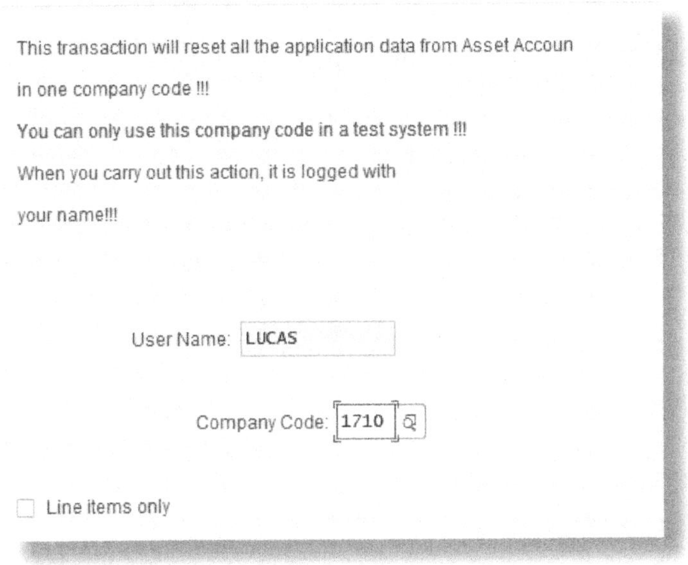

This transaction will reset all the application data from Asset Accoun

in one company code !!!

You can only use this company code in a test system !!!

When you carry out this action, it is logged with

your name!!!

User Name: LUCAS

Company Code: 1710

☐ Line items only

Figure 11.8: Reset company code

11.4.2 Execute/undo year-end closing

At some point during year end, you will need to execute the *year-end clos-ing*. But what you may not expect is that when setting up new company codes, or changing configuration for new company codes, you may need to use this during the setup of that new company code. For example, if you have copied a reference company code, or other configuration, the fiscal year for the company code may not be current. Simply execute the year-end closing to get consistent with the fiscal year needed, and consider your posting period variant settings, too. See Figure 11.9 for an illustration on how to close or reopen an asset year-end closing.

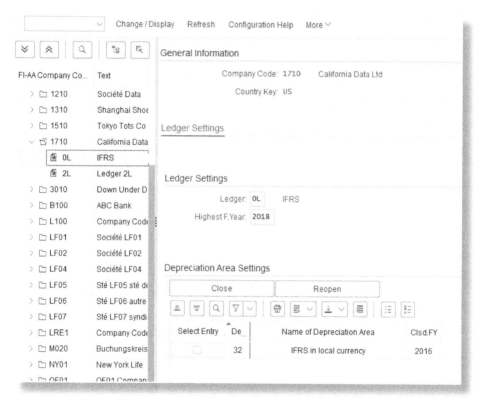

Figure 11.9: Execute or undo year-end closing

12 Overview for experts

This chapter summarizes all of the configurations that have been done up to the current point in time. This is still a dynamic node in the IMG, and will continuously be updated when configurations in other areas are updated. This is optional from the standpoint that all the items in this section are replications from other sections and nodes.

12.1 Assign accounts

Assigning the accounts is one of the most critical elements of asset accounting configuration. This overview section allows for review of the accounts that are assigned to the chart of depreciation, and for any chart of accounts that have also been used with the chart of depreciation. Remember that the chart of accounts is not dependent on the chart of depreciation. Don't forget to choose the correct chart of depreciation when reviewing the accounts and depreciation areas, as shown in Figure 12.1

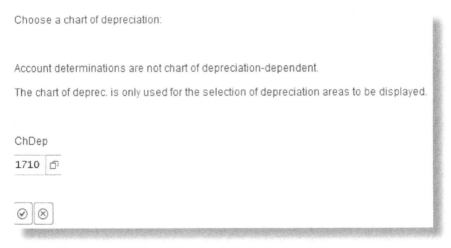

Choose a chart of depreciation:

Account determinations are not chart of depreciation-dependent.

The chart of deprec. is only used for the selection of depreciation areas to be displayed.

ChDep

1710

Figure 12.1: Choose chart of depreciation

12.2 Assign selected G/L accounts per chart of accounts

In this section, you can assign special accounts per each chart of accounts (not chart of depreciation). Figure 12.2 shows that each account can be reviewed and entered for the depreciation area and chart of accounts.

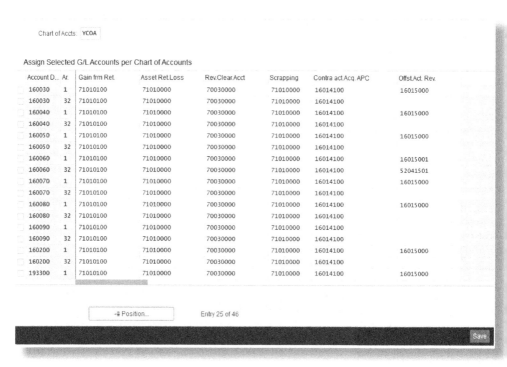

Chart of Accts: YCOA

Assign Selected G/L Accounts per Chart of Accounts

Account D...	Ar.	Gain frm Ret.	Asset Ret.Loss	Rev.Clear.Acct	Scrapping	Contra act.Acq. APC	Offst.Act. Rev.
160030	1	71010100	71010000	70030000	71010000	16014100	16015000
160030	32	71010100	71010000	70030000	71010000	16014100	
160040	1	71010100	71010000	70030000	71010000	16014100	16015000
160040	32	71010100	71010000	70030000	71010000	16014100	
160050	1	71010100	71010000	70030000	71010000	16014100	16015000
160050	32	71010100	71010000	70030000	71010000	16014100	
160060	1	71010100	71010000	70030000	71010000	16014100	16015001
160060	32	71010100	71010000	70030000	71010000	16014100	52041501
160070	1	71010100	71010000	70030000	71010000	16014100	16015000
160070	32	71010100	71010000	70030000	71010000	16014100	
160080	1	71010100	71010000	70030000	71010000	16014100	16015000
160080	32	71010100	71010000	70030000	71010000	16014100	
160090	1	71010100	71010000	70030000	71010000	16014100	
160090	32	71010100	71010000	70030000	71010000	16014100	
160200	1	71010100	71010000	70030000	71010000	16014100	16015000
160200	32	71010100	71010000	70030000	71010000	16014100	
193300	1	71010100	71010000	70030000	71010000	16014100	16015000

→ Position...   Entry 25 of 46

Save

Figure 12.2: Assign selected G/L accounts per chart of accounts

12.3 Check depreciation areas

To ensure that the chart of depreciation is configured correctly, you can review the depreciation areas in this section. If you have made any changes to the standard chart of depreciation that is delivered by SAP, you want to pay close attention to the composition of the depreciation areas here. You can review several nodes all in one section; the depreciation area definition; whether or not the area is set up for ordinary depreciation; if the area is set up for special depreciation, unplanned depreciation, transfer of reserves, interest, investment support, or replacement values; or if the cross-system depreciation areas are in use in the intracompany transfer variants. See Figure 12.3 to see an illustration on the check for depreciation areas.

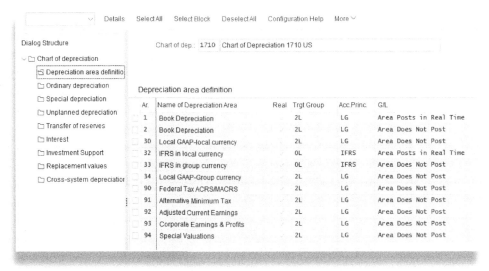

Figure 12.3: Check depreciation areas

12.4 Check real depreciation areas

Real depreciation areas post to the G/L and statistical depreciation areas are used for reporting of asset values, so you want to review them here, and make sure they are set up as intended for the chart of depreciation. You can review the chart of depreciation for area type, currency type, copy of values, copy of depreciation terms, gross value copy for intercompany transfer, sequence of depreciation calculation, and capitalization version. See Figure 12.4 for a review of the real depreciation areas.

Dialog Structure				
⌄ ☐ Chart of depreciation	Chart of dep.: **1710**	Chart of Depreciation 1710 US		
☐ Area type	Ar.	Name of Depreciation Area	Typ	Description
☐ Currency type	01	Book Depreciation	01	Valuation for trade bal. sheet
☐ Value copy rules	02	Book Depreciation	01	Valuation for trade bal. sheet
☐ Copy rules for depreciation	30	Local GAAP-local currency	01	Valuation for trade bal. sheet
☐ Gross transfer for interco. ;	32	IFRS in local currency	06	Group valuation
☐ Sequence of depreciation ;	33	IFRS in group currency	06	Group valuation
☐ Capitaliz. version	34	Local GAAP-Group currency	01	Valuation for trade bal. sheet
	90	Federal Tax ACRS/MACRS	10	US: Federal tax ACRS / MACRS
	91	Alternative Minimum Tax	12	US: ALTMIN - Alternative minimum tax
	92	Adjusted Current Earnings	13	US: ACE - Adjusted Current Earnings
	93	Corporate Earnings & Profits	14	US: E&P - Earnings & Profits
	94	Special Valuations	02	Special dep. reserves (special tax depreci…

Figure 12.4: Check real depreciation areas

12.5 Check active charts of depreciation for asset accounting

You want to review the charts of depreciation for several reasons. You want to ensure the many configuration settings are correct. You will want to review configuration settings such as layouts and account determination, because if these are not correct, they will cause you headaches later. To ensure the configuration is correct, start your review here. Enter your chart of depreciation and execute the review. If the review finds any issues with a configuration in the chart, please be sure to correct the issue before going live with the chart. Take advantage of the tool to get the system checked and ready for go live. Please see Figure 12.5 for the report results from of an active charts of depreciation check.

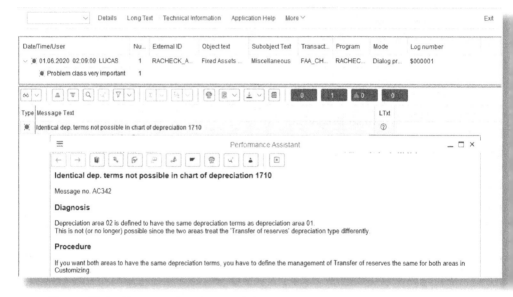

Figure 12.5: Check active charts of depreciation

12.6 Check company code

When checking the configuration of the company code, it is important to keep several things in mind for review and confirmation. You can review several items here for the company code, such as the chart of depreciation, document type for depreciation, number range, fiscal year variant, and many more, as shown in Figure 12.6.

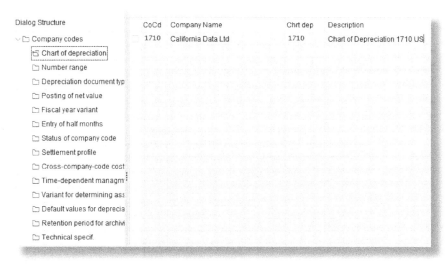

Figure 12.6: Check company codes

12.7 Check depreciation areas of company codes

In this section, you can review most of the configuration items around the depreciation areas in the company code. This is a good place to review configurations and compare with other company codes and depreciation areas. Figure 12.7 shows all the items available for review.

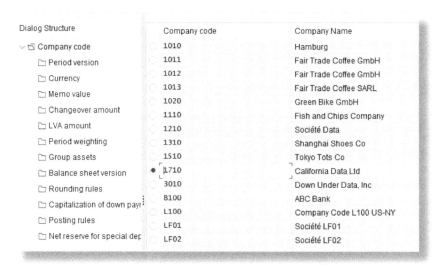

Figure 12.7: Check depreciation areas of company codes

161

12.8 Check account assignments

For areas that are posting to ledgers, you can review the account assignment configuration here. If you want to compare this transaction with another transaction, use transaction code AO90 for the account determination configuration transaction. Figure 12.8 shows where to review the account assignments.

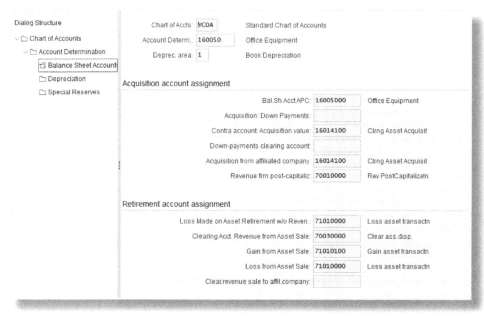

Figure 12.8: Check account assignments

12.9 Check transaction types

If you have made any new transaction types, it is important to review them here. These should have a Y or Z prefix for the naming convention of the transaction types. You can also compare and contrast the transaction types that are standard from SAP. Please see Figure 12.9 for the review of the asset transaction types.

Figure 12.9: Check transaction types

12.10 Check asset classes

Last but not least, when reviewing asset classes, you want to ensure the accuracy of the user fields, memo values, group assets, long-term templates, and many other items of configuration. Please see Figure 12.10 for an example of the asset class review.

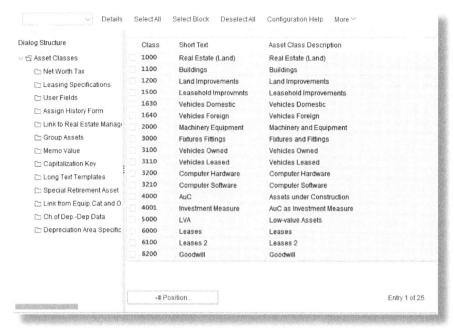

Figure 12.10: Check asset classes

13 Migration: Asset accounting (new)

The migration to the new asset accounting is complex and includes several steps, so it will be important to have experience with this exercise or seek additional help from outside your current arena if you are not comfortable or qualified to continue the migration.

You have been introduced to SAP Asset Accounting, the terminology, concepts, transactions, etc., and can now move into how to migrate asset accounting.

It is recommended that however you proceed, and with whomever you proceed, please ensure you have completed a simulated migration in a test environment or temporary environment. This effort will be thrown away after the migration, but the learning you gain can help when you proceed with the next migration. Even before you start the exercise, be sure you have read through the documentation and SAP notes recommended by SAP. Note SAP Note 1939592 is of particular importance, so ensure this has been reviewed and also any relevant notes, or versions. There are several steps in the migration process, so if you are not focused, and miss a step, it could prove to be costly and disastrous.

Another item to familiarize yourself with is that some components are not compatible with the new SAP Asset Accounting, so ensure the components have been noted and alternative measures taken, if necessary. The components are covered in the documentation and should be reviewed thoroughly.

Always be cognizant of the phrase, "Contact your local consultant." This is a very simple phrase, but it is a very important one; a good consultant will have gone through the process several times, and will be able to help you proceed with a much higher chance of success. Likewise, an inexperienced consultant will decrease your chance for success, and increase your chance for failure. So, when choosing a consultant, choose wisely. Never underestimate the need for this type of assistance; it will prove invaluable not only today, but also tomorrow and the years to come. Talk to people in the user groups, conferences, etc., and make sure you find a good consultant. Check references and do your homework.

Parallel currencies must be the same in the G/L and other ledgers, as they are in the depreciation areas.

In some cases, if you only have a single ledger, the leading ledger, you will not need to worry about other currencies and depreciation areas.

13.1 Migration from classic to new asset accounting

13.1.1 Prepare new asset accounting

In this section, there are no configuration items, but there is some heavy documentation to read through that details what needs to be done when migrating from the *classic asset accounting* to the *new asset accounting*. Please take some time here to read through the IMG activity documentation, found in the IMG node, which shares the same name as this section.

13.2 Migration for new asset accounting

Please note there are several steps to perform before you can start using the new Asset Accounting in SAP S/4HANA, and the steps must be done in sequence. You will need to do the work in your development environment first, and then transport the changes to the test and production systems.

Attention: Cannot revert to classic asset accounting

 Keep in mind, once you perform the migration to the new Asset Accounting, you cannot revert to the classic Asset Accounting.

13.2.1 Migrate charts of depreciation

This is the first step in a configuration and corresponds to SAP's fourth step in the documentation, for which there are 15 steps documented. Once this step is completed, it will not be done again in the same system. Before taking this step in the process, be sure to complete the prerequisites. These prerequisites can be found in the documentation. Ideally, you should have assigned the accounting principles to ledger groups, and also assigned a ledger and accounting principle to the company code used in the Asset Accounting that is undergoing the migration. Figure 13.1, shows that chart of depreciation 1710 is being prepared for migration with a test run.

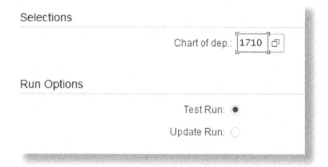

Figure 13.1: Migrate charts of depreciation

13.2.2 Display migration log

After the migration has been executed, take some time to review the logs. The logs will be generated for test and update runs, and will be saved in the system for future reference.

13.2.3 Perform additional manual activities

This step is a placeholder for manual activities that must be completed before moving on to the next configuration step. Be sure to review the documentation for delta customizing in SAP Help. There are several required and optional steps to take before proceeding to the next migration step in the configuration. Keep in mind you will have different steps to take and a different path to follow depending on if you choose the accounts approach, or the ledgers approach.

13.2.4 Check prerequisites for activating asset accounting (new)

Be sure to run the check program once you are ready to activate the new Asset Accounting in the current system. Once you have activated the new Asset Accounting, you cannot activate it again. The system knows it has been activated and will provide you with a message if you try to run this activity a second time. In Figure 13.2, you can see the new check program for Asset Accounting is activated in SAP S/4HANA.

Figure 13.2: Activation check before import

13.3 Activate asset accounting (new)

The ACTIVE setting and status is done first in the development system and saved. It can then be transported to downstream systems such as test and production. Before transporting to these downstream systems, be sure to follow the prescribed steps from SAP and check that the prerequisites have been done in each system. If they have not been performed, then the status will not be saved. Only after this status is saved as 'Active' will you be able to post in the system with the new Asset Accounting. In Figure 13.3 you can view the activation of NEW ASSET ACCOUNTING in SAP S/4HANA.

Figure 13.3: New asset accounting is active

13.4 Adjustments in new asset accounting

13.4.1 Info: Adjustments in new asset accounting

This is another placeholder for steps in the migration process to new Asset Accounting. If you have not yet made the adjustments in your system, then complete these adjustments now. Check the accounting principles, check the ledgers and ledger groups, assign accounting principles to ledger groups, check assignment of accounting principles to company code, and adjust parameters in the chart of depreciation. These steps are listed redundantly in SAP Help, so be sure to document how these steps are performed in your system for future reference. This may also be the time where you deactivate the old transaction types that will no longer be used in the new Asset Accounting.

13.4.2 Adjust parameters in chart of depreciation

This activity will accomplish two things: assign an accounting principle to a depreciation area and change the posting indicator for periodic posting. Remember there are prerequisites, such as periodic postings, that must be performed and completed before proceeding with this step. Figure 13.4 shows the TEST RUN option selected for adjusting parameters in the chart of depreciation.

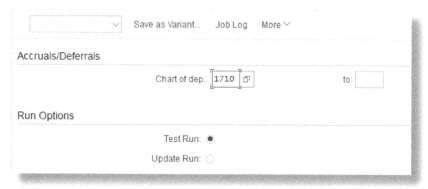

Figure 13.4: Program to adjust parameters in chart of depreciation

13.4.3 Display migration log

Take a few moments to review the logs for any errors or warnings that will signal an incomplete status. Once the chart of depreciation has migrated, you will see a successful log in this list.

Congratulations on completing the migration to new SAP Asset Accounting.

You have finished the book.

A The Author

Jerry Lucas is a seasoned SAP Asset Accounting veteran with over 20 years of experience with SAP and Asset Accounting. He was initially certified in FICO by SAP back in 1999. Throughout his career, he has been on many projects around the globe. He has traveled extensively to many countries and worked with folks with various country backgrounds. Jerry presented Asset Accounting research and findings at the 2016 SAP Financials Conference in Las Vegas. His educational background includes dual bachelor degrees in finance and information sciences, as well as a master's degree in business administration, all from the University of Florida. He currently lives in Tampa, Florida, and enjoys family time chasing his kids around, fishing, boating, being on the water, and bicycling.

B Index

C Disclaimer

This publication contains references to the products of SAP SE.

SAP, R/3, SAP NetWeaver, Duet, PartnerEdge, ByDesign, SAP Business-Objects Explorer, StreamWork, and other SAP products and services mentioned herein as well as their respective logos are trademarks or registered trademarks of SAP SE in Germany and other countries.

Business Objects and the Business Objects logo, BusinessObjects, Crystal Reports, Crystal Decisions, Web Intelligence, Xcelsius, and other Business Objects products and services mentioned herein as well as their respective logos are trademarks or registered trademarks of Business Objects Software Ltd. Business Objects is an SAP company.

Sybase and Adaptive Server, iAnywhere, Sybase 365, SQL Anywhere, and other Sybase products and services mentioned herein as well as their respective logos are trademarks or registered trademarks of Sybase, Inc. Sybase is an SAP company.

SAP SE is neither the author nor the publisher of this publication and is not responsible for its content. SAP Group shall not be liable for errors or omissions with respect to the materials. The only warranties for SAP Group products and services are those that are set forth in the express warranty statements accompanying such products and services, if any. Nothing herein should be construed as constituting an additional warranty.

More Espresso Tutorials Books

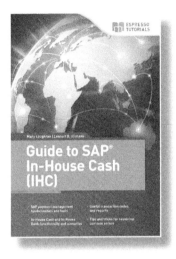

Mary Loughran, Lennart Ullmann:

Guide to SAP® In-House Cash (ICH)

▶ SAP payment management fundamentals and tools

▶ In-House Cash and In-House Bank functionality scenarios

▶ Useful transaction codes and reports

▶ Tips and tricks for resolving common errors

http://5191.espresso-tutorials.com

Mary Loughran, Praveen Gupta:

Cash Management in SAP® S/4HANA

▶ Principle areas of Cash Management powered by S/4HANA

▶ Comparison between ECC and SAP S/4HANA functionality, including an overview of release 1809

▶ Deployment options and implementation steps

▶ SAP Cash Management implementation tips and tricks

http://5281.espresso-tutorials.com

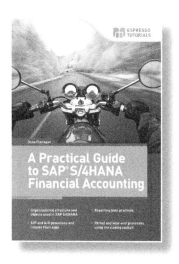

Oona Flanagan:

A Practical Guide to SAP® S/4HANA Financial Accounting

▶ Financial accounting processes in SAP S/4HANA

▶ Finance organizational structure, key financial master data

▶ Daily transactions using SAP Fiori apps

▶ SAP Fiori apps for displaying and reporting financial data

http://5320.espresso-tutorials.com

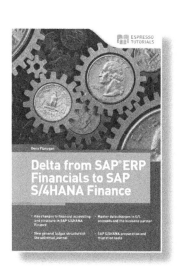

Oona Flanagan:

Delta from SAP ERP Financials to SAP® S/4HANA Finance

▶ Key changes to financial accounting and structure in SAP S/4HANA Finance

▶ New general ledger structure in the universal journal

▶ Master data changes in G/L accounts and the business partner

▶ SAP S/4HANA preparation and migration tools

http://5321.espresso-tutorials.com

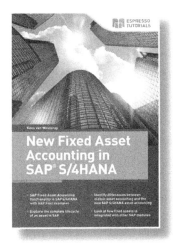

Kees van Westerop:

New Fixed Asset Accounting in SAP® S/4HANA

▶ Describes SAP Fixed Asset Accounting functionality in SAP S/4HANA with SAP Fiori examples
▶ Explores the complete lifecycle of an asset in SAP
▶ Identifies differences between classic Fixed Asset Accounting and the new SAP S/4HANA Fixed Asset Accounting
▶ Examines how Fixed Asset Accounting is integrated with other SAP modules

http://5409.espresso-tutorials.com

Maddie Allenspach:

First Steps in Financial Accounting in SAP® S/4HANA

▶ Explore key process areas in Financial Accounting in SAP S/4HANA
▶ Delve into key SAP Fiori applications
▶ Look at key SAP S/4HANA concepts such as master data,
▶ SAP Fiori screens, the universal journal, Central Finance, and reporting tools
▶ Learn how to tailor the user experience in SAP Fiori

http://5410.espresso-tutorials.com

Mary Loughran, Praveen Gupta:

Bank Communication Management in SAP® S/4HANA

- ▶ Explore BCM functionality in SAP S/4HANA and ECC, including process flows, reporting, and configuration
- ▶ Dive into the technical aspects of using BCM
- ▶ Learn about SAP Advanced Payment Management and SAP Multi-Bank Connectivi-ty
- ▶ Troubleshoot common implementation challenges

http://5469.espresso-tutorials.com

Made in the USA
Coppell, TX
15 October 2024

38699998R00105